OK, GOD, LET'S START FROM **HERE** ↓

TRICIA DRAPER

ISBN 978-1-64416-256-9 (paperback)
ISBN 978-1-64416-257-6 (digital)

Copyright © 2018 by Tricia Draper

All rights reserved. No part of this publication may be reproduced, distributed, or transmitted in any form or by any means, including photocopying, recording, or other electronic or mechanical methods without the prior written permission of the publisher. For permission requests, solicit the publisher via the address below.

Christian Faith Publishing, Inc.
832 Park Avenue
Meadville, PA 16335
www.christianfaithpublishing.com

Printed in the United States of America

To Carolyn & Don,
It has been a joy and pleasure getting to know you both. I truly love you. God will continue to bless you Always!
Tricia Draper

I would like to thank all my family and friends who have helped bring this book to publication. Without them, this would not be possible. Throughout this project, this scripture Jesus spoke has come to my heart and mind:

- Jesus looked at them and said, "With man this is impossible, but not with God; all things are possible with God." (Mark 10:27, NIV)

Contents

Foreword 7
Chapter 1: Talking 9
Chapter 2: Listen 15
Chapter 3: Authority 23
Chapter 4: Ask 31
Chapter 5: Seek/Focus 42
Chapter 6: Trust 50
Chapter 7: Stand 58
Chapter 8: Battle 64
Chapter 9: Physical and Spiritual Pain 74
Chapter 10: Relationship 84
Chapter 11: Praise 90
Chapter 12: Thanks 98
Chapter 13: Joy 106
Chapter 14: Gifts/Give 115
Chapter 15: Fun 122
Chapter 16: Goodness 127
Chapter 17: Dreams and Goals 133
Chapter 18: Love 137
Chapter 19: Take Me/Want Me 143
Chapter 20: Positive Affirmations 147

Prayer for Salvation 157
Prayer for Receiving the Holy Spirit 159
Versions of the Bible 161

FOREWORD

God is always talking; we only have to listen. He wants to have a close and personal relationship with every one of us. He loves us and wants us to know and always remember that.

When I decided to write this book, I thought that it would be about a big revelation like an *aha* moment, but God showed me that we can start from wherever we are. He is always ready for us to come to Him when we realize our mistakes and turn to Him. He waits for us to come to the end of ourselves and realize that He is the only way we can truly get anything done. Never be afraid to admit you need His help in any area of your life.

One way I communicate with God is through writing in journals. I write to Him and He answers me, and I write those words down. He has made it very clear that those words are meant for everyone! This is a ministry I have. There is nothing special about me for Him to speak to me this way. The only thing that qualifies me is that I listen and obey. In this book, I will share the words He has spoken to me for everyone. When you see the word, "you" know that God is speaking to you personally. He may speak to you in different ways, but one way He does communicate is through other people, and that is what this book is all about.

There are many scriptures to back up all that God says to me. Every section of this book is written by Him. He gives me words and I just write what I hear in my spirit. The scriptures are easily seen by bullets and indentions and always look like this:

- Scripture

The words that God has spoken through the journals are indented and look like this:

~ Words from journals

There are many different versions of the Bible quoted in these scriptures. We only see the initials by the scripture. Please see the note at the back of the book for the title of the version of the Bible.

This book is written in a format so you can read any chapter you want. It does not have to be in any certain order, but I suggest you do read it in the order I have laid out. However, you may need to hear something on a specific area in your life and you may jump to that chapter before any other one.

These words are from five different journals. A partial is from October of 2014, but most of the words are from December of 2015 to April of 2016. These dates are not too important since the words are timeless.

I thank you for reading this with an open heart and mind. Let the Spirit flow through you and give you the guidance you need. If you have any questions about the subject of this book, please visit my website, www.triciadraper.com. My husband and I have a radio ministry on the internet. You may also learn more about this content at www.themessengersradio.com. Please feel free to contact me with questions or concerns. I would love to help in any way.

At the back of this book, there are two prayers—the prayer for salvation, asking Jesus to come into your life and reign as your Lord and Savior, and the prayer for the filling of the Holy Spirit. I encourage you to pray these prayers out loud, since your words are very powerful. When you hear these words out loud, it goes from your head to your heart.

God bless you and please listen to the words spoken to you from the God of the Universe.

Chapter 1

TALKING

God is always talking. He has talked since time began. He spoke the world into existence.

- And God said, "Let there be light"; and there was light. (Genesis 1:3, AMP)

He created everything we know of, and probably much more, by just speaking it into existence. Amazing! When He speaks, everything happens.

He has not stopped talking since those first words were spoken. He spoke with Adam and Eve in the Garden He lovingly created for them. He spoke to people in different ways in the Old Testament. He spoke to Moses through a burning bush! (Exodus 3). God spoke to Moses on many occasions, in many ways and because Moses listened, God was able to use him in mighty ways.

God also spoke through prophets such as Samuel, who declared David would become king.

- Then Samuel said to Jesse, "Are all your sons here?" Jesse replied, "There is still one left, the youngest; he is tending the sheep." Samuel said to Jesse, "Send *word* and bring him; because we will not sit down [to eat the sacrificial meal] until he comes here."

David Anointed

- So Jesse sent *word* and brought him in. Now he had a ruddy complexion, with beautiful eyes and a handsome appearance. The Lord said [to Samuel], "Arise, anoint him; for this is he." Then Samuel took the horn of oil and anointed David in the presence of his brothers; and the Spirit of the Lord came mightily upon David from that day forward. And Samuel arose and went to Ramah. (1 Samuel 16:11–13, AMP)

God spoke to the prophet, Elijah, to turn the hearts of the Israelites back to God. He had told Elijah to proclaim a drought that would last for years until God's word brought rain (1 Kings 17:1). It wasn't until years later that we see how the word of God worked to bring His people back to Him.

Elijah's Prayer

- At the time of the offering of the *evening* sacrifice, Elijah the prophet approached [the altar] and said, "O Lord, the God of Abraham, Isaac, and Israel (Jacob), let it be known today that You are God in Israel and that I am Your servant and that I have done all these things at Your word. Answer me, O Lord, answer me, so that this people may know that You, O Lord, are God, and that You have turned their hearts back [to You]." Then the fire of the Lord fell and consumed the burnt offering and the wood, and *even* the stones and the dust;

it also licked up the water in the trench. When all the people saw it, they fell face downward; and they said, "The LORD, He is God! The LORD, He is God!" (1 Kings 18:36–39, AMP)

Other prophets were used by God through visions and dreams. Isaiah, Jeremiah, and Daniel were only a few that were used simply because they put their trust in God and obeyed what He said. I encourage you to look up some of the wonderful ways God spoke to the men and women in the Old Testament.

God is still talking to us today. Now that we have a New Covenant through the blood of Jesus on that cross He can speak to us personally. He speaks to us in many ways. He can speak to us in the still small voice in our heart, or through thoughts we think are our own, but are really messages from Him.

He also speaks to us through the Holy Spirit. Jesus told His disciples what they were to do when the Holy Spirit came upon them.

- "But you will receive power when the Holy Spirit comes upon you. And you will be my witnesses, telling people about me everywhere—in Jerusalem, throughout Judea, in Samaria, and to the ends of the earth." (Acts 1:8, NLT)

Since we are to be disciples even today, this is our mission too.

God also uses others to speak to us. He uses pastors and teachers to instill His words into our hearts. He can use anyone, even the people you least expect.

He definitely speaks to us through the Bible. It is called the Word of God. Everything we need is in the Bible if we just look close enough. Answers can always be found in the Book He gave to us.

He is always talking. One way He speaks to me is through my writing in journals. I write to Him and He talks back to me. I don't hear an audible voice, although if He wanted to do that, He could. I just feel His words in my Spirit, hear His heart, and write what I hear.

God makes it very clear that the things I am writing are not just for me. They are for everyone and that is what this book is about. These may be words written from me, but they are words straight from God to your heart. Here are some of the things He says about talking to Him and His talking to you. These are all from different journal entries.

- I am always talking so just listen.

- I am always talking and I am full of answers to all your questions. I love to reveal Myself to you and My plans for your life when you seek Me and Ask Me with your whole heart!

There is much more where this came from, but these are some of the ones He had me show you right now. He is very adamant that He is always with us and always talking. The thing we have to do is listen!

- Remember I'm always speaking. It's you who have to listen.

- I am always talking, but you must always be listening. Tune Me in and the world out.

God is not just talking; He is also listening. He loves it when we talk to Him. He says He loves communicating with us.

- I love communicating with you any way you will let Me. I love talking to you. I love listening to you. I love you writing down My words. I love it all.

He loves to hear from us. Any problem you are facing, take it to God and talk to Him about it. Any questions? Talk to Him about it. He is the only One with the correct answer every time. We need to learn to come to Him first and just talk to Him about anything. Nothing is too big for God to handle. Nothing! And He loves it! He loves answering our questions and He loves just hearing from us.

Talking to God might seem daunting to you if you have never done it. Prayer is in essence just talking to God. If you have never stopped and thought about talking to God, you should; it is very easy! You can do it anyway you feel comfortable. You can talk out loud. You can pray in your head. You can write on paper. As long as you are getting your thoughts intentionally to Him then it is considered talking to God. This is what He encourages.

~ Talk to Me all the time.

One special way to talk to God is through the gift of tongues. When we are filled with the Holy Spirit, this is one of the ways we can communicate with God. The words you speak may be in a language you don't understand, and that is fine because that is your spirit talking straight to God. That is what happened to the disciples on the Day of Pentecost as we see in Acts.

The Holy Spirit Comes

- On the day of Pentecost all the believers were meeting together in one place. Suddenly, there was a sound from heaven like the roaring of a mighty windstorm, and it filled the house where they were sitting. Then, what looked like flames or tongues of fire appeared and settled on each of them. And everyone present was filled with the Holy Spirit and began speaking in other languages, as the Holy Spirit gave them this ability. (Acts 2:1–4, NLT)

In the next few scriptures we see that people from different lands heard them and understood what they were saying in their own language, but this is not always the case. It doesn't matter if you understand the words; the point is your spirit is praying perfectly to the one true God.

There may be certain ways you have learned to pray to God and that is fine, as long as you talk to Him from your heart. As long as your faith allows, you can talk to God anywhere at any time.

I encourage you to stop reading right now and take a moment to just say something to God. If you can't think of anything, just simply say, "Thank You!" "Thank You" are two of the greatest words you could say to God. He has blessed us so much and many times we forget to say it. You like it when people say "thank you" to you and God loves it too.

The best words I think you could ever say are "I love You!" Those words fill His heart and when you say them, just realize He is saying the same thing back to you. In every single journal entry, from the first to the most recent, He has said "I love you" more than once. This is how He feels and exactly what He is saying to you right now.

When things start piling up in my mind and I realize I haven't taken time to talk to God, I just say, "OK, God, let's start from here."

Chapter 2

LISTEN

Listening is not just hearing with your ears. It is hearing with your heart. Understanding comes with true listening. Sometimes we spend too much time talking, and we don't listen enough. Wars can be started with words but avoided with listening. When we truly put others first, then we can learn more about who they are and who we need to be in Christ. We can learn what they need so we can help them in their journey with God. We are meant to edify others only, not to speak harsh words and hurt others. Paul tells the Thessalonians this very thing.

- So encourage each other and build each other up, just as you are already doing. (1 Thessalonians 5:11, NIV)

In a letter to the Ephesians, Paul talks about the words of your mouth and how they are to be used to help one another.

- Let no corrupt communication proceed out of your mouth, but that which is good to the use of edifying, that it may minister grace unto the hearers. (Ephesians 4:29, KJV)

When we listen more, we hurt less. We can hurt ourselves less and we can hurt others less just by listening to what is said. Men are often accused of "not listening" like many women feel they should. Women are often accused of talking too much, therefore, not being able to really listen. The truth is that it depends on the person. Many people, men and women, are so caught up in their own lives and things of this world that they don't take the time to listen with their whole heart to what other people are saying.

I don't want to group together men vs. women, but science has found that men are created with different genes than women. I find they tend to react differently than women because they hear a problem and want to "fix" it. Women have genes that tend to nurture and want to help the person who needs the problem fixed. These two differences are in no means the way every man and woman react to things, but knowing this, we can see how some cases of listening and reacting to problems can be construed as underwhelming or overwhelming.

For example, Jessica has a problem with a co-worker, and she just needs someone to listen to her hurting heart. She explains this situation to Debra, who listens and tells her everything will be okay, if she just lets it go and gives it to God. Jessica's friend Allen hears about the problem and goes to the co-worker explaining that things need to change where Jessica is concerned.

Both of Jessica's friends have only her best interest at heart, but the way they go about helping her is very different. While Jessica may need to vent to Debra, she also needs to hear reassurance from her. Allen, although trying to help, may have "fixed" the problem, or he may have made it worse. The point is they both listened.

So when we feel someone isn't listening, they actually may be, but they may be processing it in their own way. We need to be listening and lifting others up. Debra could have been talking to Jessica about other things in her own life and not taken the time to really listen to Jessica, but only heard her words. Allen may not have been listening to Jessica and not bothered to do or say anything to help alleviate her problem. We need to listen more and speak less. We need to listen to understand, not just to reply.

- My dear brothers and sisters, take note of this: Everyone should be quick to listen, slow to speak and slow to become angry, because human anger does not produce the righteousness that God desires. (James 1:19–20, NIV)

Sometimes people don't even have to speak for you to listen to what they are saying. When someone is hurting, if you pay attention, you don't have to hear them speak before you know there is something wrong. Sometimes the things people don't say are louder than what they do say. In these cases, we need to hear with our heart and help in any way we can.

One of the ways I communicate with God is through a journal. I talk to Him and then I write down what He has to say to me. He tells me things for everyone to hear and understand. They are teaching tools and lessons that we all need to know. He says this several times throughout my journals.

~ I am always here to listen. You know you can always come to Me.

~ I am always talking, but you are not always listening.

We need to not only be hearers of the Word but doers also. James warns his listeners about this.

- Do not merely listen to the word, and so deceive yourselves. Do what it says. Anyone who listens to the word but does not do what it says is like someone who looks at his face in a mirror and, after looking at himself, goes away and immediately forgets what he looks like. But whoever looks intently into the perfect law that gives freedom, and continues in it—not forgetting what they have heard, but doing it—they will be blessed in what they do. (James 1:22–25, NIV)

God explains it this way in the journal.

- You are doing much better at asking, but now we need to work on listening and putting it into practice. Even when you listen you may not always obey. Obey is the lesson of the day. It is the lesson of every day!

- Keep your eyes on Me and listen and obey. You need to do what I say, when I say it. Don't stop to think. Just listen to Me and jump. When you are trusting Me and doing what I say, no harm will befall you.

- You have to obey to get to bigger trust levels.

- You cannot get good results if you won't listen to My answers.

Often when we get into battles, physical or spiritual, we may hear God, but we don't really listen. When we need Him the most, we need to get alone with Him and listen to how He wants us to fight the battle. Reading His Word and praying to Him are not the only ways we can get things done. We have to come to the point where we listen and obey His commands.

Now, sometimes we have to go around the mountain (our problem), so to speak, several times before we give ourselves over to God and listen to Him to find the answer to our problem. Wouldn't it be great if we could just do that in the first place? That should be the goal for every believer. It's all about our relationship with Him. Wherever we are in our walk with God, He wants us to be closer. He longs for an intimate relationship with us. He wants to tell us things, wonderful things, but we have to be listening to understand them. This is how He puts it in a journal entry.

- I will show you wonderful things but you must ask Me to understand them and put them into perspective. Remember, garbage in, garbage out. So watch what you put into your mind and spirit. Think on pure and lovely things. Think on Me and listen to what the Spirit is saying to you. You need to listen and obey.

He gives us a good recipe to help us fight our battles.

- Ask Me and listen. Don't get depressed or lose that joy! You are fighting in a battle that you must win. Pray without ceasing. Build yourself up in your most Holy Faith.

Sometimes we just don't feel like listening to God. We may not be saying that in those words, but by whining and complaining all the time, we are saying that we don't want to listen to God. I don't mean that we cannot vent our feelings, but we need to go to God after we do. We can tell Him anything from our highs to our lows. He wants to hear them from us, but He also wants us to listen to what He has to say in order to help us.

I was in the middle of a battle at one point and had another session where I was complaining to God. "Why, God?" It's a question we ask so many times in the midst of our struggles. Then I realized I was questioning God and that made me stop and think. Was I whining too much? Was I just not listening to God? I started to write in my journal and this is what He said.

- I don't mind answering the same questions over and over if you are willing to listen and do what I say. It's hard to answer the same questions over and over when you aren't listening—truly listening and obeying. Never stop asking; that is not at all what I am saying. Just listen and obey.

So I started to listen to Him better and even though it took a while to fight that battle I came out on top, but only when I truly stopped and listened to what He wanted me to do.

Jesus taught that He was the Good Shepherd and that we as His children are His sheep.

- "I am the good shepherd; I know my sheep and my sheep know me—just as the Father knows me and I know the Father—and I lay down my life for the sheep. I have other sheep that are not of this sheep pen. I must bring them also. They too will listen to my voice, and there shall be one flock and one shepherd. The reason my Father loves me is that I lay down my life—only to take it up again. (John 10:14–17, NIV)

Sheep are interesting little creatures. They are very dumb according to our standards, but one thing they do is listen. If a stranger tries to lead a sheep away from a flock it will not usually go. It listens to its shepherd's voice. Jesus used this example of how we are with Him. When we are His sheep (believers), we will listen to Him and answer His call.

- The one who enters by the gate is the shepherd of the sheep. [3] The gatekeeper opens the gate for him, and the sheep listen to his voice. He calls his own sheep by name and leads them out. [4] When he has brought out all his own, he goes on ahead of them, and his sheep follow him because they know his voice. (John 10:2–4, NIV)

We may wander away from the flock on our own and if we do, the devil is just lying in wait, ready to gobble us up as a lion would a sheep. He is the master deceiver and we are made susceptible when we are not with our flock (other believers following Jesus). But Jesus made a wonderful promise to us in a parable He taught while He was on this earth.

- So Jesus told them this story: "If a man has a hundred sheep and one of them gets lost, what will he do? Won't he leave the ninety-nine others in the wilderness and go to search for the one that is lost until he finds it? And when he has found it, he will joyfully carry it home on his shoulders. When he arrives, he will call together his friends and neighbors, saying, 'Rejoice with me because I have found my lost sheep.' In the same way, there is more joy in heaven over one lost sinner who repents and returns to God than over ninety-nine others who are righteous and haven't strayed away! (Luke 15:3–7, NLT)

When I was younger, that verse always seemed like He didn't care about the ninety-nine he left behind, but that is not the truth at all. He loved the ninety-nine so much that He knew they could be trusted with keeping themselves together. He knew He could go after that one sheep because it needed Him at that moment more than the ninety-nine. If it were any one of the other ninety-nine, He would have done the same thing for them. He trusted His sheep to listen to His voice.

We find that God is always talking, and we must always be listening; not just hearing. We need to be that way with everyone. I encourage you to take time to listen to those around you. Make it a point to stop the craziness in your world for a while and just focus on what a loved one is saying. Show someone you care about that you love them enough to just listen and help if need be. It will give you a sense of understanding that you did not have before.

Make it a point to sit down with God and do the same thing. Ask Him your questions, tell Him how you feel, rant and rave if you must, but then stop and listen. Listen to what He is telling you because He is always telling you something. Open your heart and listen. Then obey what He tells you. Even if He only tells you He "loves you," obey Him by accepting that fact and remembering it when you go throughout your day.

Everything comes down to your relationship with God and listening is the beginning of any good relationship. This is something He is saying to you right now.

> ~ Listen. Listen intently to what I say. I say you are Mine. You are My beloved. You are a child of the Most High God! You are more than your feelings.

God showed me this in a journal and I believe it is a very trustworthy saying.

> ~ The best teachers are listeners and the best listeners are teachers. You must be both.

We need that special relationship with God. When I find myself getting too caught up in my own issues and not asking God or listening to Him, I take the time to go talk to Him and say, "OK, God, let's start from here."

Chapter 3

AUTHORITY

Authority. It does us no good if we do not know we have it. It is like a man who has a million dollars in the bank but doesn't know it, so he is living on the streets. He has the money at his disposal, but he doesn't even know what he has. That is how so many of us are with the authority we have in Jesus's Name. Jesus died to give us the authority He had. Jesus knew He had the authority from God, His Father, as we see in these verses.

- I don't speak on my own authority. The Father who sent me has commanded me what to say and how to say it. (John 12:49, NLT)

- Jesus knew that the Father had given him authority over everything and that he had come from God and would return to God. (John 13:3, NLT)

Jesus had the Holy Spirit on the inside of Him, working all the time. Jesus had *all* the authority, in heaven and earth and under the earth, and He knew it. He walked it out. It was a free gift given to Him by His Father. He knew who He was and whose He was.

Jesus sent out the disciples in Matthew 10, Mark 6, and Luke 9. We find He gave them the power they needed to heal the people they came in contact with. He had the authority from God to send them.

Jesus Sends Out the Twelve

- When Jesus had called the Twelve together, he gave them power and authority to drive out all demons and to cure diseases, and he sent them out to proclaim the kingdom of God and to heal the sick. (Luke 9:1–3, NIV)

Not only did Jesus send out the twelve disciples, in Luke 10, He sent seventy-two more out with the same power and authority. The disciples were given the command to not only heal, but let the people know that the Kingdom of God was at hand.

- Heal the sick who are there and tell them, "The kingdom of God has come near to you." (Luke 10:9, NIV)

A perfect example of Jesus explaining this authority is found in Matthew 16.

- I will give you the keys (authority) of the kingdom of heaven; and whatever you bind [forbid, declare to be improper and unlawful] on earth will have [already] been bound in heaven, and whatever you loose [permit, declare lawful] on earth will have [already] been loosed in heaven." (Matthew 16:19, AMP)

One of the last things Jesus gave the disciples was the authority to go into all the world and give their authority to others. This is called the Great Commission found in Matthew 28.

OK, GOD, LET'S START FROM HERE

The Great Commission

- Then the eleven disciples went to Galilee, to the mountain where Jesus had told them to go. When they saw him, they worshiped him; but some doubted. Then Jesus came to them and said, "All authority in heaven and on earth has been given to me. Therefore, go and make disciples of all nations, baptizing them in the name of the Father and of the Son and of the Holy Spirit, and teaching them to obey everything I have commanded you. And surely I am with you always, to the very end of the age." (Matthew 28:16–20, NIV)

That is authority! You know you have authority when you can give it to others. It's like a person who is in charge of other people, such as a boss at work. They have been given authority by the company, but you have no authority until they give it to you. Let's say it this way, God is the head of all "the Company." He (the company boss) gives authority to someone to lead and rule the people (Jesus). Then, the leader (Jesus) uses His authority to help you. Let's say, that leader died and you obtained his job at work. Now the company (God) gives you all the authority the other leader had (Jesus). The point is you have the authority that Jesus had and died to give you.

You may think, "Yeah, but that was for the disciples back then. I don't have that kind of power!" That is where you are wrong. Not only do you have that authority, but you can show others how to use their authority by teaching them what the Bible says. When Jesus told the disciples to "go and make other disciples," that includes you and me. We have everything they had. This commission is not a suggestion. This is what we are made for. We were made to use our authority in Jesus's Name and go into all the world. That may seem like a big task, but Jesus said we would do even greater things than He did.

- Very truly I tell you, whoever believes in me will do the works I have been doing, and they will do even greater things than these, because I am going to the Father. (John 14:12, NIV)

Jesus knew what authority He had. We, as believers, need to find that authority and use it. If you are a believer, then you need to first and foremost understand that you are a child of God. We are His children just as Jesus was His child. God endowed Jesus with power and authority. Jesus, in turn, gave it to us.

Here are some examples of what your authority can do. Several years ago, I started having pain in my right shoulder. I stood on this promise from the Word of God.

- "He himself bore our sins" in his body on the cross, so that we might die to sins and live for righteousness; "by his wounds you have been healed." (1 Peter 2:24, NIV)

Jesus died to give me this healing and I have known that since I was a child growing up in a Christian home. So I stood on that word and believed I would be healed. The truth is that I was healed that day on that cross. It's very important to realize that our manifestations come in different ways and at different times. We are all already healed by Jesus's stripes, but healings come in different forms and fashions. Just because your healings manifest in one way, but not another, doesn't mean that you are doing something wrong. This is a tricky area where the devil loves to confuse everyone. The truth is that God *never* harms you or makes you sick to teach you a lesson. Your body is born of this earth and is subject to decay, unless you take your stand and live your faith by the Word of God. In Deuteronomy 34:7, it states,

- Moses was 120 years old when he died, yet his eyesight was clear, and he was as strong as ever. (Deuteronomy 34:7, NLT)

Moses was strong in his faith and knew God wanted him to prosper in every way, even physically. God works in many ways; through miracles, steadfastness, and even doctors and medicines. God meets you where your faith is. The important part is that He has already healed you and He always wants you well.

We have authority over every area of our lives, including healing our bodies, but we have to stand up and use it. I did this one night with my shoulder pain. After I had tried other methods of healing, I got mad and took a stand against the devil. I had heard enough lies from him about how much pain I was in and how I had to stay that way. I took my authority Jesus had given me and I spoke out loud, rebuking that pain. I said, "Enough is enough! I do *not* have to take this pain! In Jesus's Name, I have authority over this body and I command it healed and whole! I will not let you (satan) have control *anymore* in Jesus's Name! Thank You, Jesus, for dying to give me this authority. I love You! Thank You! Amen!" Right at that moment, I saw my healing. I had full range of motion that I did not have before and no pain.

Using your authority is an everyday battle. As soon as you do take your stand and use your authority, the devil will come to challenge you. The day after I spoke my authority over my arm, I woke up with a sore shoulder. I could easily have given up hope and believed that I wasn't really healed, but I was not going to let satan steal my blessing. I said, "No! I am healed and whole in Jesus's Name! Nothing is going to take that from me. I have the authority." I could hear satan whispering in my ear that I was not really healed, but I knew that old trick. I put him right in his place . . . under my feet (Romans 16:20). I had to counterbalance those negative thoughts with praise for the One who gave me my authority; my precious, precious Jesus. I started to praise God and I forgot all about everything else. My spirit was filled with joy and I had a wonderful day!

Here are some of the things God spoke to me, through my journal, during this time in my life. You may be in the same type of painful situation as I was, so please know that these words are just as much for you as they were for me.

- I love you and I'm not impartial to your pain. It hurts Me to see your body not lining up with My Word. But you need to use your Authority. Use Me!

- I hate to see you in pain when you don't have to be. Use your Authority and put My Name to good use.

- You have that Authority at a high price, so treat it as such. You think you are in pain now, but it is nothing compared to dying on a cross! I'm not shaming you. You are feeling pain, but you can't let it take hold of you. Come to Me and let Me fight this battle. I already defeated it! I will win this battle with you at my side.

He also encourages us to use His authority in every area of our lives.

- Think of Me and lay everything else aside. Turn to Me All the time—not just when you are in need. Use your Authority, that I died to give you, and take control—not over just your body, but your circumstances, too. You have power for every part of your life. Put Me in control to lead you, but you must use the power I give you to walk it out. I tell you to follow Me and you do, but you must have My power to do that. You must use Me. I am the only way you will get anything done, ever. Period.

Obviously, we can get things done, on our own, when we don't ask for His help, but usually we mess things up. The point He was trying to make is that we can't get things done the way they need to be done without Him.

We not only have His authority when we are in need, but we have the authority of His Name to help others.

- If you don't know who you are, how will you show others what they can be?

- Take your Authority and trust Me! Use My Name—that is why you know it. I gave it to you so you could use it.

- Remember the authority I have given you and *use* it. I have not just given you the authority to heal, but to have power in everything you do in My Name.

I think it is important to point out that we have the authority to use His Name, but that doesn't mean we can get whatever we want when we use it. It must line up with His Word. Using His Name is a way of using our faith. It is putting our trust in Jesus and letting our spirit agree with His. This is all for His Glory and to see His Kingdom come, like He mentioned to the disciples in Luke 10:9. It's not only about healing or having our needs met, but also supporting Him and agreeing with all that He is.

We are in good company when we use His authority. Many people in the Bible had to learn to use it too. This is what He said about that in my journal.

- The closer you come to Me, the closer I will come to you. I promise. It worked for all the believers in the Bible, pre- and post-covenant. Many people did many things in My Name and were rewarded handsomely. But each one of them had to learn who they were in Me and how to use My Authority. Some learned quickly, but others took a while.

In scripture, we see that under the Old Covenant, the Holy Spirit could not rest on the people for long, because they were not righteous. The Holy Spirit came on Moses when he parted the Red Sea, but could not stay with him the whole time. Under the New Covenant, Jesus gave us this righteousness so that we can have the Holy Spirit's power working through us all the time. That is where we get our power to use the authority Jesus gave us in His Name.

Here is something we have to look forward to when we believe until the very end.

- And he who overcomes [the world through believing that Jesus is the Son of God] and he who keeps My deeds [doing things that please Me] until the [very] end, to him I will give authority *and* power over the nations; 27and he shall shepherd *and* rule them with a rod of iron, as the earthen pots are broken in pieces, as I also have received *authority* [and power to rule them] from My Father. (Revelation 2:26–27, AMP)

So now that we have seen His authority in operation throughout the Bible, we need to learn more about it. We can never learn too much of God. Jesus died to give us the authority of His Name. He did this so we could, in turn, go out and live it. We can use it in every area of our life and then turn around and teach others how to use it. When I realize I need a new revelation of the power of this authority, I simply say, "OK, God, let's start from here."

Chapter 4

ASK

    Ask. It is something we are taught to do from the time we are little. When my son was little, we used to say, "Use your words." He knew he should not let us know what he wanted by pointing to something and whining. He did not get anything that way. He had to learn to open his mouth and ask us for what he wanted. Asking God for our needs and desires is something He encourages us to do throughout the Bible. Let's look further into this subject.

- This is the confidence we have in approaching God: that if we ask anything according to his will, he hears us. And if we know that he hears us—whatever we ask—we know that we have what we asked of him. (1 John 5:14–15, NIV)

- Very truly I tell you, whoever believes in me will do the works I have been doing, and they will do even greater things than these, because I am going to the Father. And I will do whatever you ask in my name, so that the Father may be glorified in the Son. You may ask me for anything in my name, and I will do it. (John 14:12–14, NIV)

Many of us ask God for something, but we don't think He has ever answered. He will always answer, but we may not understand Him. He has a different perspective than we do. God knows what is best for us. So what we think are unanswered prayers, could just be the best things for us.

- You desire but do not have, so you kill. You covet but you cannot get what you want, so you quarrel and fight. You do not have because you do not ask God. When you ask, you do not receive, because you ask with wrong motives, that you may spend what you get on your pleasures. (James 4:2–3, NIV)

Joyce Meyer, a Christian speaker and teacher, explains it this way:

"James summarizes the whole situation in one sentence: "You do not have, because you do not ask." Essentially, he points to how we try to get things ourselves instead of asking God for them.

You may think, "But I *have* asked God for things; He just has not given them to me."

If you ask God for something and He does not give it to you, the reason is not that He is holding out on you. It may be that it is not His will or that now is not His time. It may be that there is something better He wants to give you, but you are not yet spiritually mature enough to have it. Whatever the reason, it is never because He does not want you to be blessed.

You are God's child, and He loves you. He is a good God Who only does good things, and He wants to do for you so much more than you could possibly imagine (see Ephesians 3:20). But He loves you too much to give you something that is going to hurt you. He loves you too much to give you things that will ultimately make you more carnal or more fleshly or that may even drag you into sin because you are not yet ready to handle them.

Does a loving parent give his children the keys to the car before they are old enough to drive? Of course not, because the parent knows they may get hurt in a wreck through their inexperience. God is the same way with His children. Because He loves us, He will not give us something before we have the spiritual maturity to handle it.

I have discovered that the secret of being content is to ask God for what I want and to rest in the knowledge that if it is right, He will bring it to pass at the right time. If it is not right, He will do something much better than what I asked for." (Joyce Meyer, *The Everyday Life Bible* (New York: Faith Words, 2006) page 2068)

This doesn't mean we should stop asking God for the desires of our heart. He loves to bless us and see us succeed. One way God does this is through answering our prayers.

When we ask, sometimes we need to do so out loud. God knows our hearts, and He knows what we need before we do, but words are very powerful. We need to speak the words out loud because we need to hear it ourselves. It will build our faith. Also, God is a gentleman, and He will not always work in our lives until we ask Him. This does not mean that He will never do anything to help us without our asking, but He needs our faith to complete the task. Jesus tells us in Matthew 7:7–11, Mark 11:23–25, and Luke 11:10–14 what we need to do to receive from God.

- "Ask and it will be given to you; seek and you will find; knock and the door will be opened to you. For everyone who asks receives; the one who seeks finds; and to the one who knocks, the door will be opened. "Which of you, if your son asks for bread, will give him a stone? Or if he asks for a fish, will give him a snake? If you, then, though you are evil, know how to give good gifts to your children, how much more will your Father in heaven give good gifts to those who ask him!" (Matthew 7:7–11, NIV)

He has told me a few things concerning this area.

- Ask Me what needs to be done, because I can't just tell you everything. You need to care enough to listen and receive. If you don't care enough to ask, then you won't care enough to do. Ask. Seek. Knock.

- Ask and you shall receive, I promise. Maybe not as you expect, but you will get the right desires from the right heart.

- You have to trust Me with control of your life. I am a gentleman and I will never take over what is not given to Me. You have to give Me your life to control, in order for Me to do so. I need your permission. I need you to Ask! Don't take for granted that I can just help out whenever I want. I have to be asked!

- You prayed in tongues today and I heard the desires of your heart. But you have to ask Me with your mouth. You know how important words are! So Ask for your desires and listen for My answer.

- Ask Me out loud for the desires of your heart. We both need to hear them. Keep your dreams in front of you always. Keep your dreams alive and Dream Big. I AM a Big God who loves to have fun and I have lots of fun blessing you and enjoying your praise and worship. I love it when you talk to Me, no matter where or when. I love hearing you and being included in your day.

Even in the Bible, people had to ask out loud. Jesus needed the people to ask Him to heal them. They needed to use their faith to ask. Sometimes they had to do this very persistently. We see this in Luke 18:35–43.

- As Jesus approached Jericho, a blind man was sitting by the roadside begging. When he heard the crowd going by, he asked what was happening. They told him, "Jesus of Nazareth is passing by." He called out, "Jesus, Son of David, have mercy on me!" Those who led the way rebuked him and told him to be quiet, but he shouted all the more, "Son of David, have mercy on me!" Jesus stopped and ordered the man to be brought to him. When he came near, Jesus asked him, "What do you want me to do for you?" "Lord, I want to see," he replied. Jesus said to him, "Receive your sight; your faith has healed you." Immediately he received his sight and followed Jesus, praising God. When all the people saw it, they also praised God. (Luke 18:35–43, NIV)

Actions are also a way of asking. Many people in the Bible asked Jesus for healing by showing their faith in their actions. We find a woman, with the issue of blood, showing great faith in Mark 5:25–34.

- A woman [in the crowd] had [suffered from] a hemorrhage for twelve years, and had endured much [suffering] at the hands of many physicians. She had spent all that she had and was not helped at all, but instead had become worse. She had heard [reports] about Jesus, and she came up behind Him in the crowd and touched His outer robe. For she thought, "If I just touch His clothing, I will get well." Immediately her flow of blood was dried up; and she felt in her body [and knew without any doubt] that she was healed of her suffering. Immediately Jesus, recognizing in Himself that power had gone out from Him, turned around in the crowd and asked, "Who touched My clothes?" His disciples said to Him, "You see the crowd pressing in around You [from all sides], and You ask, 'Who touched Me?'" Still He kept looking around to see the woman who had done it. And the woman, though she was afraid and trembling, aware of what had happened to her, came and fell down before Him and told Him the whole truth. Then He said to her, "Daughter, your faith [your personal trust and confidence in Me] has restored you to health; go in peace and be [permanently] healed from your suffering." (Mark 5:25–34, AMP)

In Mark 2:3–5 we find that the faith of friends even counts as faith to Jesus. We all need to have friends like this!

- Then they came, bringing to Him a paralyzed man, who was being carried by four men. When they were unable to get to Him because of the crowd, they [a]removed the roof above Jesus; and when they had dug out an opening, they let down the mat on which the paralyzed man was lying. When Jesus saw their [active] faith [springing from confidence in Him], He said to the paralyzed man, "Son, your sins are forgiven." (Mark 2:3–5, AMP)

OK, GOD, LET'S START FROM HERE

God is not hiding from you. He wants to bless you and reveal His plans for your life. This is what He says.

- Keep asking and searching. I told you; you would find Me. I'm not hiding. I'm just waiting for you to come to Me. I can't just come to you until you are ready.

- I'm not hiding. I'm *in* you. Ask Me. Ask Me for your heart's desires. Your heart desires the things of My heart.

- I am always talking and I am full of answers, to all your questions. I love to reveal Myself to you and My plans for your life, when you seek Me and Ask Me with your whole heart!

- Keep your focus on Me. I have all the answers you seek. Ask Me, like you are doing now, and listen. You will hear Me in the still small voice in your heart.

- I will guide your steps if you will ask Me and allow Me to work through you.

It is very important to remember that when you ask, you must truly believe. Ask with a faith-filled heart. There are a couple of Bible verses that comment on this.

- Jesus replied, "Truly I tell you, if you have faith and do not doubt, not only can you do what was done to the fig tree, but also you can say to this mountain, 'Go, throw yourself into the sea,' and it will be done. ^{22} If you believe, you will receive whatever you ask for in prayer." (Matthew 21:21–23, NIV)

- If any of you lacks wisdom, you should ask God, who gives generously to all without finding fault, and it will be given to you. But when you ask, you must believe and not doubt, because the one who doubts is like a wave of the sea, blown and tossed by the wind. (James 1:5–6, NIV)

He wants us to ask Him for more of our hearts desires. Joyce Meyer again, teaches in The Everyday Life Bible:

"There are two ways to handle problems—the natural way and the spiritual way." James 1:5–6 tells how to solve your problems the spiritual way. It says if you have trouble, simply ask God what you should do. You may not receive an answer immediately, but you will find that divine wisdom (wisdom beyond your natural understanding) will begin to operate through you, helping you know what to do." (Joyce Meyer, *The Everyday Life Bible* (New York: Faith Words, 2006) page 2060)

God says in the journal:

~ Ask for more wisdom and insight.

We are disciples of Christ and we are supposed to not only go into the world, but also to be fruitful, meaning that we show God in our lives. We know that trees are fruitful when we see an apple tree full of apples or an orange tree ripe with fresh fruit. Jesus tells us that God wants us to bear good fruit. He shows us this concept in John.

- If you do not remain in me, you are like a branch that is thrown away and withers; such branches are picked up, thrown into the fire and burned. If you remain in me and my words remain in you, ask whatever you wish, and it will be done for you. This is to my Father's glory, that you bear much fruit, showing yourselves to be my disciples. (John 15:6–8, NIV)

- You did not choose me, but I chose you and appointed you so that you might go and bear fruit—fruit that will last—and so that whatever you ask in my name the Father will give you. (John 15:16, NIV)

We often say a prayer and then walk away expecting God to do all the work. Then, we wonder why nothing happens. Sometimes we just need to ask and let Him explain things to us. He is the One who tells us what we need to know, so we must listen and understand.

- Ask! I want to explain, but you must ask and listen.

- I will show you wonderful things, but you must ask me to understand them and put them into perspective. Remember, garbage in, garbage out. So watch what you put into your mind and spirit. Think on pure and lovely things. Think on Me and listen to what the Spirit is saying to you. You need to listen and obey.

There is joy in asking God for your needs. Jesus tries to comfort His disciples by explaining this. They may not have understood at the time, but they did when these truths happened.

- So with you: Now is your time of grief, but I will see you again and you will rejoice, and no one will take away your joy. In that day you will no longer ask me anything. Very truly I tell you, my Father will give you whatever you ask in my name. Until now you have not asked for anything in my name. Ask and you will receive, and your joy will be complete. (John 16:22–24, NIV)

God is pleased and happy to give us the desires of our hearts. He does not begrudgingly give us what we ask. But it is our responsibility to ask. We cannot expect to receive before we even ask.

- It is your responsibility to seek Me and Ask Me what you need and when. It is My responsibility to look after you and come near to you when you come near to Me. Let Me take care of you. I love to do it! It makes Me happy to please you and take care of you when you Ask Me to and put Me in control.

- I love being the "Daddy"—the One who fixes all your problems. Just let Me. Ask Me and let Me!

- Keep asking!

It is also very important to thank God. I think this is one of the most underrated areas in the Christian life today. Even when we say our prayers before we eat, we thank Him. But do we do so with a truly thankful heart, or are we just repeating the same words over and over again? It is fine to say the same things repetitively, but it's all about what is in our heart. We should always have a heart of gratitude. It not only pleases Him, it lifts our heart, and brings our spirit to life. He says concerning this:

- But you ask and I love to answer. And then, you thank Me! Wow! It makes it even more joyous. You make My heart sing. I have angels who sing to Me all the time, but when you thank Me and let Me in, it is more wonderful than all of Heaven!

OK, GOD, LET'S START FROM HERE

Now that is how I want God to feel all the time. I want to please Him and draw near to Him all day, every day. This seems to sum up how I feel.

- One thing I have asked of the Lord, and that I will seek: That I may dwell in the house of the Lord [in His presence] all the days of my life, To gaze upon the beauty [the delightful loveliness and majestic grandeur] of the Lord And to meditate in His temple. (Psalm 27:4, AMP)

I'm not saying I'm there yet, but I am better than I was. When I do mess up I know I have a loving Father who is always there to help me start over again. I can truly say, "OK, God, let's start from here."

Chapter 5

SEEK/FOCUS

When I was little, I played a game called hide-and-seek. I'm sure many of you did too. One person hid while to other one "sought." The person was to seek or look intently to find the other person who was hiding. It was great to look since you knew it meant you were good at finding someone and proved how great you were at the game. There was only one problem: I felt disappointment when I looked and did not find. It propelled me to keep on looking but it was a setback. But when I did find the person, it was so exciting! I felt a sense of accomplishment and fulfillment. It was a win for me.

Now that I am grown, I am realizing that we, as people, are too often playing a game of hide-and-seek in life. Many of us are looking for fulfillment, but we don't find it in any place we look in the world. We search and search but cannot seem to fill that void inside of us. It's quite honestly frustrating.

Then somehow, we hear about our loving God and His Son, Jesus. So since we are so used to playing hide-and-seek to get what we want, we try to play that with God. The problem with that is that God is not hiding. He is right in front of us, holding His arms open wide, ready for us to run into them and let Him take all our cares and problems. So many people out there today don't know He is ready to receive every part of us, including our guilt, shame, sin, and all the yucky stuff that comes with those things. He just honestly and perfectly loves us. All He wants is for us to believe and acknowledge Him. He is never far from us as we see in Acts.

- God did this so that they would seek him and perhaps reach out for him and find him, though he is not far from any one of us. (Acts 17:27, NIV)

God may not be hiding, but He knows we are seeking for an answer to fill that void in our lives. He knows we must seek with our hearts to find Him and His perfect will for our lives. Thankfully, He promises us in His Word (the Bible) that when we do seek, we will find.

- "Ask and it will be given to you; seek and you will find; knock and the door will be opened to you. [8] For everyone who asks receives; the one who seeks finds; and to the one who knocks, the door will be opened. (Matthew 7:7–8, NIV)

This verse promises us that when we do seek, we will find. There is a carefully laid out set of instructions He has set up for us to follow. When we follow these instructions, He will be there to answer us, and guide us through this crazy life.

One way I communicate with God is through a journal. I talk to Him and He speaks back to me. I write down what He says. The words in these journals are meant for you too. He has this to say in one of them.

- Come, seek Me and you shall find. Come close to Me and I shall come close to you. I love you. Never doubt or forget that.

- Keep asking and searching. I told you, you would find Me. I'm not hiding. I'm just waiting for you to come to Me. I can't just come to you until you are ready.

~ I am always talking and I am full of answers to all your questions. I love to reveal Myself to you and My plans for your life, when you seek Me and ask Me with your whole heart.

Just as in the game, hide-and-seek, we have to actively look for God's will. He never moves so we are not seeking Him but His will. To do this, we have to put our faith into action. This means doing something on our part. As in the verse, we need to ask. For more on this subject, see the Ask section of this book. When we ask we must then show our faith by taking a step and looking to find His will. He explains this better in the journals.

~ You have to look—to do something of your own accord—to find Me.

~ Seeking is somewhere you go, not something that just happens. It takes effort on your part.

~ Don't pull away or half-heartedly seek Me. Put your all into everything you do for Me. Live Me to the fullest. Love Me. Love Me more that you think you are capable of.

The Bible shows us some more insights on seeking God.

- Seek *and* deeply long for the Lord and His strength [His power, His might]; Seek *and* deeply long for His face *and* His presence continually. (Psalm 105:4, AMP)

- But if from there you seek the Lord your God, you will find him if you seek him with all your heart and with all your soul. (Deuteronomy 4:29, NIV)

- Seek his will in all you do, and he will show you which path to take. (Proverbs 3:6, NLT)

God himself said in this next verse a promise that I feel is much needed today in our world. This is something we, as His children, must actively seek Him and do.

- If my people, who are called by my name, will humble themselves and pray and seek my face and turn from their wicked ways, then I will hear from heaven, and I will forgive their sin and will heal their land. (2 Chronicles 7:14, NIV)

Our world has fallen into disrepair and we as a body of believers need to join together and take back the promises God has given us to be victors in this world. He tells us that we are not only to seek Him but to seek Him first.

- But seek ye first the kingdom of God, and his righteousness; and all these things shall be added unto you. (Matthew 6:33, KJV)

This is a precious promise we have from Him. He tells us that if we lay ourselves down and actively seek, we will reap benefits of His love and the things we need. He talks about this in the journal.

~ Seek Me first and last.

~ Seek Me first *and* all these things shall be added unto you. Remember the rest of the promise. It is just as important as the first.

- Seek Me first! And all these things will be added unto you. If you seek, you will reap the benefits of this promise.

- Seek Me first. It means come to Me first in every and all situations. Me. I am first. Troubles, questions, lessons, praises—all to Me first. Then, listen and let Me teach you. If it is something bad then you tell Me and we will work on it together. And if it is good I want to be the first One to hear about it.

God wants us to seek Him all the time not just when it is convenient for us. Sometimes we may not feel like seeking Him but that is usually when we need Him the most. Here are some words from Him in the journal.

- Don't get discouraged. Keep seeking Me and keep walking forward.

- You need to seek Me even when your defenses are down.

- Seek Me in times of trouble and in times of prosperity.

God loves us and longs for us to come closer to Him. He wants us to seek so we will find. He wants us to dream and be happy about seeking Him. He doesn't want it to be hard for us or a burden. He wants us to do it joyfully and He will bless us in return. The Bible expresses this.

- Glory in his holy name; let the hearts of those who seek the Lord rejoice. Look to the Lord and his strength seek his face always. (1 Chronicles 16:10–11, NIV)

- The poor will eat and be satisfied. All who seek the Lord will praise him. Their hearts will rejoice with everlasting joy. (Psalm 22:26, NLT)

He encourages us in the journal.

- I long to show you all I can do, but you can't understand and you won't if you don't seek Me first and dream bigger. Let Me show you how awesome I really am!

Sometimes when we are in the middle of seeking God, we can lose our focus if we are not careful. We are our weakest when we are walking through a storm or trial in our lives. The devil knows this and loves to do what he does best and tries to confuse us in hopes of making us lose our focus when we are trying to seek God. We just need to remember to keep our focus and look up to God and give Him our worries and cares. He wants to take them and give us hope in return. Here are some things He says about staying focused.

- You have to calm your mind down to hear My voice. When you have so many thoughts, you can't focus. You have to focus and seek Me to hear Me. I speak in quiet voices so you are really paying attention. I have your full cooperation when I have your attention.

- It is hard to focus but it will always be. There is never a time when you will not be distracted by the world. The enemy will always come against you.

- Now is the time to focus on Me and don't look down at the waves. It's chaos and easy to sink, but let Me pull you out as soon as you ask!

- Don't ever get overwhelmed or get lost in your thoughts. You know satan loves to whisper in your ear to take your focus off of Me. Just seek Me first and put one step in front of the other. One step at a time.

- If you have no focus you will get nowhere.

It is important to remember that we are to seek God, not man. Sometimes we hear a certain preacher or speaker, and it is easy to put them up on a pedestal. But they are only people and while we can learn from them and take advice, we have to seek only God. We are to follow Him and His will for our lives. Just as we saw in Matthew 7:7–8 we are to ask to find His will and then seek His answer. After that, when we knock, the door will be opened and we will have our answers. Remember, this is a process and while some answers we will get quickly, we may have to seek harder on others. We just can't give up when we seek. We have to trust and take a step of faith. God explains more in the journal.

- Don't seek after anyone else. Just Me. Thank you for trusting Me and stepping out in faith. It may seem scary, but when you take your eyes off your circumstances, you won't doubt at all. When you look to Me, I direct your steps and everything goes smoothly.

We find in the Bible that faith is very important to Him. We as believers have to have it in order to get anything accomplished. We are to trust and have faith as it says in Hebrews.

- And it is impossible to please God without faith. Anyone who wants to come to him must believe that God exists and that he rewards those who sincerely seek him. (Hebrews 11:6, NLT)

OK, GOD, LET'S START FROM HERE

I must admit that when I started working on this subject of seeking God, I got a little overwhelmed on what exactly it was all about and how to do it right. I was seeking Him and earnestly asking what He wanted to say through me about the subject. One night, He spoke these words to me and I hope they will simplify the subject for you too.

- I don't want you to become overwhelmed by something so easy. It is not hard to seek My face. Just ask and trust. Read My Word and trust. Thank Me and trust. Follow Me and trust. Turn from your old ways and trust. Do you see the pattern? Yes, you have to do something but most importantly, trust!

- Many (people) are wondering "how" to seek My face and what all that entails. It is different for different people but in all situations, they must empty themselves and fill up with Me.

So we find that when we sincerely seek, even through the tough times, we will find Him and be rewarded. I believe when we seek joyfully, we will reap more benefits. It is easier to seek His face when we give up all of ourselves and let Him take over. When we surrender, the Holy Spirit will lead and guide us. God is pleased when we seek Him wholeheartedly.

When I find myself losing focus or not seeking as I should, I remind myself that He is always near and I need to seek His will above mine. That's when I say, "OK, God, let's start from here."

Chapter 6

TRUST

Trust is one of the most important parts of our walk with God. If we don't trust Him, it will be a hard journey, and we will miss out on so much. If we don't trust, we could have anxiety, fear, and suffering, among other unpleasant feelings. But if we do trust in God, we will have peace, love, joy, and all the other inspiring gifts of the Lord.

Some companies nowadays have trust exercises to help their employees learn to rely on each other. One person closes their eyes and falls backward. The other people are behind to catch them, showing that the person's trust was successful. This is a good exercise to do with the people around us, but we must do this with our spirit and God. That is what faith is. Faith is taking a step out with no safety net and trusting God to "catch" us.

Trusting, believing, and faith go hand-in-hand. We cannot believe if we do not have faith and trust in God. We cannot have faith without trusting and believing God. And we cannot trust in God if we don't believe and have faith that He is even there.

Trust is first. If we don't trust that God will help us, then we will not believe that anything will get done. If we don't believe, we have no faith. When we trust, we can believe that God will do what He says. Then we can step out in faith and trust that God will be there to help us on our journey.

The Bible says that we are to trust God with everything we have.

- Trust in the Lord with all your heart and lean not on your own understanding; in all your ways submit to him, and he will make your paths straight. (Proverbs 3:5–6, NIV)

Some of the Words God has spoken to me through a journal are meant for everyone. Here are some of the things He says about trusting completely with all of ourselves.

~ Trust Me with your thoughts, your feelings and your heart.

~ When you don't trust completely, you don't give Me your whole heart. You keep some back, and that is where the enemy strikes. He knows he can't touch the part that you entrust to Me, but when he plants that sliver of doubt, he can get to all your heart if you are not careful and don't trust. Don't give him a way in. Guard your heart. Trust Me with all of it. Don't hold anything back.

~ I need you to do the work I created you for. I need your complete surrender and your complete trust.

The book of Psalms is full of people professing their trust in God and urging others to do so as well. Here are some examples.

- [*Psalm 25*] [*Of David.*] In you, Lord my God, I put my trust. (Psalm 25:1, NIV)

- But I trust in you, Lord; I say, "You are my God." (Psalm 31:14, NIV)

- In God I trust and am not afraid. What can man do to me? (Psalm 56:11, NIV)

The Bible tells us that God is our strength and our fortress. Fortress is a word that basically means He is a safe place for us. Imagine back in the older days when a city was all surrounded by thick stone walls. This was to protect them from the enemy. That is why the Bible says God is our fortress because He surrounds us and protects us from the enemy.

- I will say of the Lord, "He is my refuge and my fortress, My God, in whom I trust [with great confidence, and on whom I rely]!" (Psalm 91:2, AMP)

- The Lord is my rock, my fortress, and the One who rescues me; My God, my rock *and* strength in whom I trust *and* take refuge; My shield, and the horn of my salvation, my high tower—my stronghold. (Psalm 18:2, AMP)

The Bible also explains that God is our refuge. He is a safe place for us to dwell. He longs for us to simply trust in Him and rest in His mighty, capable hands. He wants us to feel safe and secure. Imagine Him wrapping His arms around you to hold you and protect you from harm.

- Trust in him at all times, you people; pour out your hearts to him, for God is our refuge. (Psalm 62:8, NIV)

- But as for me, it is good for me to draw near to God; I have made the Lord God my refuge *and* placed my trust in Him, That I may tell of all Your works. (Psalm 73:28, AMP)

- Every word of God is tested *and* refined [like silver]; He is a shield to those who trust *and* take refuge in Him. (Proverbs 30:5, AMP)

- The Lord is good, a refuge in times of trouble. He cares for those who trust in him. (Nahum 1:7, NIV)

- How precious is your unfailing love, O God! All humanity finds shelter in the shadow of your wings. (Psalm 36:7, NLT)

In the journal, He tells us to give up all control of ourselves to Him. Here are a few passages.

- I want what is best, but you have to give up control and let Me work. Trust Me. Just relax in the Shadow of the Almighty—Me!

- You have to trust Me with control of your life. I am a gentleman, and I will never take over what is not given to Me. You have to give Me your life to control in order for Me to do so. I need your permission. I need you to Ask! Don't take for granted that I can just help out whenever I want. I have to be asked!

- I love you and I will not let you go astray when you trust Me and put Me in control. Put Me first and leave Me there! I love you and I want to be the One you want.

God not only wants us to give Him our trust, He wants us to do so joyfully. This may seem like a hard thing to do at first, but when we truly give up our cares and concerns, it gets easier to trust Him. Each step we take of completely trusting and believing gets easier and easier. We have more faith to help us trust him more and more.

- The Lord is my strength and my shield; my heart trusts in him, and he helps me. My heart leaps for joy, and with my song I praise him. (Psalm 28:7, NIV)

- Those who listen to instruction will prosper; those who trust the Lord will be joyful. (Proverbs 16:20, NLT)

- In that day they will say, "Surely this is our God; we trusted in him, and he saved us. This is the Lord, we trusted in him; let us rejoice and be glad in his salvation." (Isaiah 25:9, NIV)

- May the God of hope fill you with all joy and peace as you trust in him, so that you may overflow with hope by the power of the Holy Spirit. (Romans 15:13, NIV)

There are several journal entries about being joyful and trusting in not only the good times, but the bad ones too.

- ~ Trust. Rejoice in Me always—especially when things are going wrong. That's when I am hard at work. That's when the good comes out; in the trials. Don't let your flesh weigh your Spirit down.

- ~ You need to trust Me in the good times and the bad. Remember Whose you are.

> ~ Don't worry about anything. Trust in Me Always! I am Jehovah Jirah—your provider. I will always take care of you and I love to bless you. It makes Me happy to see you happy. I love to give good and precious gifts to My children.

There are different levels of trust. In some situations, we are able to easily trust that God can and will do what He says in a certain area, but sometimes it's harder to believe right away. This has to deal with our personal walk with Him. A friend might be believing for the same breakthrough that you are, and they are confident and assured, while you are left wondering and slow to trust. Maybe that person has already dealt with a situation like this before and they are ready to trust due to their success last time. You may never know. It is *all* about the relationship each of us has with God. We are on a daily walk with Him, and where we are can determine the trust we have. A journal entry reaffirms this.

> ~ If you are focused on it (the problem) and don't give Me a chance to help you, you are not going to trust Me enough. If, however, you look to Me and give Me all your cares and concerns, then you can easily trust.

Trust is a give and take with God. He trusts us more when we trust Him more. We can show we are trustworthy by our belief, faith, and trust in Him. He explains it this way in the journal.

> ~ You trust in Me and I trust in you. It's a give-give situation. It's like a see-saw. You give, I give.

> ~ I'm trusting you. Show Me you are trustworthy. Believe you are. You are meant for more than you are right now.

This does not mean that God will never trust you before you do something for Him. He knows your heart and knows what you are capable of before you even do. He knows how great you can be, and He trusts that you want the best for yourself, and that includes Him. We may not see it in ourselves, but God does. He made you with the gifts and talents you have, so you could not only enjoy them, but also use them to further His Kingdom.

Sometimes we trust and believe, but don't see things happen right away. This is when we need to trust Him the most, because something great is more than likely coming our way. It seems that the longer the time we have to wait on His response, the greater the answer is for us. God has His own timetable and we are not privileged enough to know it. It could actually be harmful to us to know what will take place because we could hurt ourselves trying to do something on our own that only God can do. We could mess up the wonderful plans God has for us. He reminds us of this very thing in the journal.

- Trust me and seek Me. Things happen in My timing and you must trust that. I am never late. I am always on time.

We have a basic outline to follow to receive from God. It says in Mark 11:23–24 and James 1:6 that if we believe and do not doubt, we will receive what we ask for, according to His will. Remember, you have to trust to believe. So we ask, trust, believe, and we will receive. He shows us this concept in the journal.

- Ask, trust, believe, and you shall receive.

- Trust Me to give you what you need when you need it. Everything else is already yours, so claim it. Believe and receive! Name it. Call it out of your mouth.

OK, GOD, LET'S START FROM HERE

He makes an important point in the entry above. We have to not only trust, but we need to speak out with our mouths the things we ask. The spoken word is so very important. You can change lives for the better or worse with the words of your mouth. You speak into existence what is or is not. See the section on Talking in this book for a more in depth study of this concept.

We need to trust and do not doubt, as the Bible tells us. We need to find a way to trust in God for the answers we are seeking. We are to put our full trust in Him, knowing that He not only will answer us, but that He wants to do so. He loves to answer us, even if we don't like the answer. God has only the best for us. We are His beloved and He longs to give us the desires of our heart, not only for our benefit, but for His glory also.

He said this in a journal entry and it really got me thinking. I realized there is more to this trust issue than I originally thought. See what you think.

~ Trust Me, but trust the Me in you.

As believers, we need to trust that He is inside of us, helping us make the right decisions. We don't always realize it is Him who is nudging us in the right direction. We need to trust that He is always with us and will never leave us or forsake us as it says in Deuteronomy.

- Be strong and courageous. Do not be afraid or terrified because of them, for the LORD your God goes with you; he will never leave you nor forsake you." (Deuteronomy 31:6, NIV)

When I find myself lacking in trust in any area of my life, I apologize to God and ask for His help. I take a breath and say, "OK, God, let's start from here."

Chapter 7

STAND

When I think of standing strong, I think of a showdown at the OK Corral. Imagine two people standing across from each other just staring one another in the eye. The two are very intent. The air is still—no breeze at all. There is a line drawn in the sand. There are no guns in this battle, just sheer will. It is a dare. Who will flinch first? Will one of them back down and step over the line?

That is how it is with satan and us sometimes. Jesus has drawn the line in the sand, showing us how we should live and directing our paths. But satan is standing on the other side, staring at us, trying to get us to back down and take one step across that line. Sometimes we may not be strong enough and we take that step. Don't worry, we have all done it, and we all will at some point, because we are not perfect. But God has blessed us and does not punish us when we are not strong enough. He just leans down and draws another line, giving us another chance.

He tells us in James 4:7 a remedy to stand firm against satan and how to make him run in terror.

- So submit to [the authority of] God. Resist the devil [stand firm against him] and he will flee from you. (James 4:7, AMP)

Paul shows us a recipe for standing against the enemy.

- Put on all of God's armor so that you will be able to stand firm against all strategies of the devil. For we[a]are not fighting against flesh-and-blood enemies, but against evil rulers and authorities of the unseen world, against mighty powers in this dark world, and against evil spirits in the heavenly places. Therefore, put on every piece of God's armor so you will be able to resist the enemy in the time of evil. Then after the battle you will still be standing firm. Stand your ground, putting on the belt of truth and the body armor of God's righteousness. (Ephesians 6:11–14, NLT)

In the NIV verse 13 says it this way. I like this one because it is straightforward, and I remember it easier.

- Therefore, put on the full armor of God, so that when the day of evil comes, you may be able to stand your ground, and after you have done everything, to stand. (Ephesians 6:13, NIV)

They are both great scriptures and they help us when we do slip up and lose our step. With God's help, we are then able to stand again. We get back up and stand. When we have tried to do everything on our own and failed, we have to rely on God to help us stand back up for Him.

I communicate with God on different levels, as many of us do. One way is that when He speaks to me, I write it down in a journal. These words are intended for everyone, not just me. That is what this book is about. These are His words to you. In one entry He said,

- Stand and when you have done all you can, stand.

In another entry, He explained that we need not only to stand, but to stand on the decisions we make. We need to stand up for what we believe.

- Trust Me and stand. When you have done all you can, stand! Well, don't wait until you have tried everything else! Stand now! Take a stand and own it. Make a decision and go for it. I have told you—if you take a stand and own it, even if it is not My will—if you do it unto Me, I will honor that. We will just start from there. I honor you and your decisions. That's why you have to make your own decisions. You have to be the one who answers for them. You get the reward and you get the revision.

Don't worry about God not being there for you. He promises us that He will never leave us or forsake us. He will never let us be tempted beyond what we can bear.

- The Lord himself goes before you and will be with you; he will never leave you nor forsake you. Do not be afraid; do not be discouraged." (Deuteronomy 31:8, NIV)

- No temptation has overtaken you except what is common to mankind. And God is faithful; he will not let you be tempted beyond what you can bear. But when you are tempted, he will also provide a way out so that you can endure it. (1 Corinthians 10:13, NIV)

God knows we will stumble and fall, but He loves us and is always there for us. We find many reassurances from the Bible that give us hope for standing firm.

- He lifted me out of the slimy pit, out of the mud and mire; he set my feet on a rock and gave me a firm place to stand. (Psalm 40:2, NIV)

- You will be hated by everyone because of me, but the one who stands firm to the end will be saved. (Matthew 10:22, NIV)

- Stand firm, and you will win life. (Luke 21:19, NIV)

- Be on your guard; stand firm in the faith; be courageous; be strong. [14] Do everything in love. (1 Corinthians 16:13-14, NIV)

These scriptures give us faith to realize that no matter what happens, when we stand with God, we will finish strong with Him. God reminds us in the journal that He has given us what we need to stand firm.

> ~ You must stand and fight. Fight every battle by using what I have given you—My Word!

One important thing to know is exactly what to stand against. When we go through battles, it helps if we know our enemy, so we can be more equipped to beat him. This is an entry that talks about this.

> ~ You must know what you are standing against to truly stand. You can stand blindly, and sometimes that is what needs to be done, but you need to know the arrows the enemy is throwing at you. Your Shield of Faith will stop those, but you must be prepared, knowing how to thwart the enemy's arsenal. You can fight better if you know his

strategies. I know and I am helping you, but you are the one who has to stand and stand firm.

We know our enemy is the devil. The Bible says that he comes at us with flaming arrows (Ephesians 6:16). It also warns us that he comes only to steal, kill and destroy as we see in the book of John.

- The thief comes only in order to steal and kill and destroy. I came that they may have *and* enjoy life, and have it in abundance [to the full, till it overflows]. (John 10:10, AMP)

The last part of that verse is a wonderful promise we have from Jesus. He came to bring life to us! He promises us not only a little life but abundant life! I like how it says that we can enjoy our lives. We, as His children, are to have fun in this life. We need to enjoy our journey with God. You can see more on this in the Fun section of this book.

God is unmoving. When He promises us something, He means it and will never take it back. He gave us His Word and that is unshakable. It will stand firm to the end. These verses remind us of that truth.

- But the Lord's plans stand firm forever; his intentions can never be shaken. (Psalm 33:11, NLT)

- I will declare that your love stands firm forever, that you have established your faithfulness in heaven itself. (Psalm 89:2, NIV)

- But God's truth stands firm like a foundation stone with this inscription: "The Lord knows those who are his," and "All who belong to the Lord must turn away from evil." (2 Timothy 2:19, NLT)

OK, GOD, LET'S START FROM HERE

God's Word promises us that He will provide for all our needs. He feeds even the birds of the air, and they are not His beloved children (Matthew 6:26). He tells us in the journal:

> ~ I am your Provider. I will make you more than a conqueror! Stand with Me and nothing can stand against you. When I am on your side, who can be against you? What can man do? Man cannot conquer Me, for I have overcome the world!

With God on our side, we have faith that we can stand strong. He is there when we prosper and when we fall. He is always there for us, ready to pick us up and get us back on our feet. He lovingly helps us stand so we can do so by relying on Him for strength. We cannot stand in our own power. We are not strong enough but, with God, all things are possible (Matthew 19:26).

When I find myself stepping over that line in the sand, unable to stand under the weight of this world, I look to God for help. He picks me up and I can only say, "OK, God, let's start from here."

Chapter 8

BATTLE

We are in a battle every single second of every single day. We may not be fighting physically, like our wonderful and much appreciated soldiers, but we fight spiritual wars. We battle the enemy (satan) and his forces every day. His battlefield is in the mind. If he can get our minds off of God and onto ourselves, then it opens the door and gives him a foothold to reach into our lives. When we focus on ourselves he twists the truth and deceives us into believing the lies he has for us. He has already set into motion our destruction from the very beginning of our lives. He wants us to fail. He wants us to worship him and his world over God and His truth. He will do whatever it takes to ruin our relationship with our loving, Heavenly Father.

Paul tells us in Ephesians 6 more about this subject and what we can do to stop it.

The Armor of God

- In conclusion, be strong in the Lord [draw your strength from Him and be empowered through your union with Him] and in the power of His [boundless] might. Put on the full armor of God [for His precepts are like the splendid armor of a heavily-armed soldier], so that you may be able to [successfully] stand up against all the schemes *and* the strategies *and* the deceits of the devil. For our struggle is not against flesh and blood [contending only with physical opponents], but against the rulers, against the powers, against the world forces of this [present] darkness, against the spiritual *forces* of wickedness in the heavenly (supernatural) *places*. Therefore, put on the complete armor of God, so that you will be able to [successfully] resist *and* stand your ground in the evil day [of danger], and having done everything [that the crisis demands], to stand firm [in your place, fully prepared, immovable, victorious]. So stand firm *and* hold your ground, HAVING [a] TIGHTENED THE WIDE BAND OF TRUTH (personal integrity, moral courage) AROUND YOUR WAIST and HAVING PUT ON THE BREASTPLATE OF RIGHTEOUSNESS (an upright heart), and having [b]strapped on YOUR FEET THE GOSPEL OF PEACE IN PREPARATION [to face the enemy with firm-footed stability and the readiness produced by the good news]. Above all, lift up the [protective] [c]Shield of Faith with which you can extinguish all the flaming arrows of the evil *one*. And take THE HELMET OF SALVATION, and the Sword of the Spirit, which is the Word of God. (Ephesians 6:10–17, AMP)

There are many important topics in these verses. First he tells us that our fight is not only physical.

- For our struggle is not against flesh and blood [contending only with physical opponents], but against the rulers, against the powers, against the world forces of this [present] darkness, against the spiritual *forces* of wickedness in the heavenly (supernatural) *places.*

This verse gives us an example of who our enemy is. We cannot just get physically fit and blow up the devil with a hand grenade, as much as we would like to. Our war is mainly Spiritual. We do fight physically, but we will discuss that later.

Paul also mentioned being strong in the Lord.

- In conclusion, be strong in the Lord [draw your strength from Him and be empowered through your union with Him] and in the power of His [boundless] might.

Through this statement, he is preparing us for the next set of things we can do to help us fight this battle.

- Put on the full armor of God [for His precepts are like the splendid armor of a heavily-armed soldier], so that you may be able to [successfully] stand up against all the schemes *and* the strategies *and* the deceits of the devil.

The armor is the key to helping us stand. In the NIV version of Ephesians 6:13 it says,

- Therefore, put on the full armor of God, so that when the day of evil comes, you may be able to stand your ground, and after you have done everything, to stand. (Ephesians 6:13, NIV)

I like this because it reminds me that no matter how I stand, if I fall, all I have to do is stand on His promises again. I have the power and authority to stand strong in God's Word and His promises. I can fight the enemy by just standing and trusting in God's Word.

Paul goes on to explain what our armor is and how to use it. I use the Amplified Bible here because it seems to explain in detail about what we have.

- So stand firm *and* hold your ground, HAVING [a] TIGHTENED THE WIDE BAND OF TRUTH (personal integrity, moral courage) AROUND YOUR WAIST and HAVING PUT ON THE BREASTPLATE OF RIGHTEOUSNESS (an upright heart), and having [b]strapped on YOUR FEET THE GOSPEL OF PEACE IN PREPARATION [to face the enemy with firm-footed stability and the readiness produced by the good news]. Above all, lift up the [protective] [c]shield of Faith with which you can extinguish all the flaming arrows of the evil *one*. And take THE HELMET OF SALVATION, and the sword of the Spirit, which is the Word of God.

I have heard many teachings on why the armor goes in this order. Personally, I feel that as long as I have all these pieces together, I put them on in a way I remember. Every morning and evening I pray to reinforce my armor. I don't ever want to be without my armor, so I just reinforce it by praying over it again.

I start with the Helmet of Salvation and go down my body. I pray against negative thoughts trying to come against me. Then, I do the Breastplate of Righteousness. I pray for protection for my heart. I pray that it grows. I pray that I water the seeds of my dreams that He has placed in my heart, and cultivate them, and see the harvest. Next, I pray for the Belt of Truth. I confirm that it surrounds me always. It protects the very core of my being. It also protects the rivers of life giving water flowing from me.

After that, I pray for the peace, purpose, and prosperity that protect my feet. I know the verse says it is the peace of the readiness of the gospel, but I feel these three together are effective in getting the peace I need. My purpose is to follow God's will for my life, when I do that, I have perfect peace. I pray for prosperity in every area of my life. All three of these work together to ready me for taking the gospel to the world.

Afterward, I pray for the Sword of the Spirit, which is God's Word. This Sword is found in the Bible and what He has spoken into my life. I pray to use it in the right way, at the right time. Lastly, but not at all the least, I pray for the Shield of Faith. I confess I walk by faith and not by sight. I have recently decided that I want to be on the offensive with this armor and not the defensive. I want to go into this battle by taking on this fight and pursuing the enemy with all I have. I want to go against the darkness and push it back. After all, light wins and we are the light of the world!

God tells it this way in the journal. These are words meant for everyone.

- You are in a battle right now, but if you keep your armor on and seek Me first, you will always come out the victor!

This is just how I pray and is in no means the only way to pray. You have to decide how you put your armor on and how you use it. We have been given the proper utensils, but we have to know how to use them the way they work best for us. No one else is fighting your battles, except God, and He will fight with you according to your faith. You will use these components in the way your faith decides to use them.

As I mentioned before, we are also in a physical battle. Satan uses our physical bodies against us. Our bodies are made of flesh and blood, and are subject to decay. The enemy tries to cause sickness and disease to throw our attention, again, off of God. He tries to shift our focus. But we have authority over our bodies and we can bring them back into order, because God gave us this promise in Jesus:

- He personally carried our sins in His body on the cross [willingly offering Himself on it, as on an altar of sacrifice], so that we might die to sin

> [becoming immune from the penalty and power of sin] and live for righteousness; for by His wounds you [who believe] have been healed. (1 Peter 2:24, AMP)

Jesus died for our sins, but also for our sicknesses. He died to heal all our iniquities. He gave us the authority over our bodies to heal them and see us recover from anything the world or the devil tries to come against us with. For more information on this, read the section about authority. So while our physical battles should be short lived, it doesn't always happen that way. We will be healed according to our faith. Sickness is a weapon satan uses against us, just to take our eyes and trust off of God. While this is a physical battle, we win it through the Spirit.

What are some of the ways I can actively fight these battles, you ask. Well, I'm glad you did! There are several ways to combat these wars, but two of the best ones are prayer and praise.

Prayer, which is basically just talking to God, is encouraged throughout the Bible. Some of my favorite verses include

- Rejoice always, pray continually, give thanks in all circumstances; for this is God's will for you in Christ Jesus. (1 Thessalonians 5:16–18, NIV)

This is our family verse. I think we, as Christians, do not always have the level of joy that we need to have. Jesus did an amazing thing on that cross and we should be happy about it. Not only should we be joyful, but we should pray continually. Prayer is a means of communication with our loving Father and Creator. We tell Him how we feel and He tells us the things we need to hear. One way He speaks to us is in a still small voice in our hearts. And we always need to be thankful. He has done so much for us and we should spend the rest of our lives thanking Him. He is due that honor. When we love someone, we thank them for all they do. It is no different with God.

In Ephesians, we find Paul speaking on prayer.

- With all prayer and petition pray [with specific requests] at all times [on every occasion and in every season] in the Spirit, and with this in view, stay alert with all perseverance and petition [interceding in prayer] for all[d]God's people. And *pray* for me, that words may be given to me when I open my mouth, to proclaim boldly the mystery of the good news [of salvation], for which I am an ambassador in chains. And *pray* that in *proclaiming* it I may speak boldly *and* courageously, as I should. (Ephesians 6:18–20, AMP)

Paul knows how important it is for believers to pray. It lifts our spirits and gets us closer to God. Then he asks for prayer for himself, because having other believers agree and pray for you is important. The Bible says,

- For where two or three gather in my name, there am I with them." (Matthew 18:20, NIV)

The Ephesians may not have been with Paul in person but they were with him in Spirit. They agreed together and prayed for him. We are like Paul today. We are ambassadors of Christ. We need prayer for ourselves to proclaim boldness of speech and courage to go out and speak it. Paul was in chains, but he still knew he could further the gospel. Most of us are not in physical chains like he was, but many of us are in Spiritual chains. We need to pray for ourselves, and have other faith-filled believers agree with us, that we will have the boldness and confidence to take the gospel to the world.

Prayer needs to be consistent. It is something we always need to do. It needs to be a main part of our lives. However, this only depends on where we are in our walk with God. Many of us pray differently, according to our faith, and that is fine. If you believe you have to pray in a certain physical fashion, then you may not be able to do that all the time, but your heart should be in it every time you do pray. If you believe you are connected with God only at certain times, then be sure to put all your faith in those times of prayer. If, however, you believe that your spirit is connected with God at all times, you can pray at all times and get to a place where you can pray anywhere, at any time, without mental involvement. When you have a faith filled heart you can talk to God anyway you want.

In my Bible, which is an older version of the NIV, it says in Jude 20,

- But you, dear friends, build your selves up in your most holy faith and pray in the Holy Spirit. (Jude 20)

Some versions have "pray continually in the Holy Spirit" and I like that too. But there is something I like about this firm statement. It is as if I can hear Jesus telling me what to do to stand firm in these times of need. It gives me a clear picture of what to do. Many people do not believe in praying in the Holy Spirit, but for those of us who do, this is a clear directive.

In the journal, He encourages us:

- Win the battle through Me. Give Me your cares and concerns.

Praise is another mighty weapon in our arsenal against the enemy. Author and pastor's wife Lisa Bevere has written several books and one of them is entitled *Girls With Swords: How to Carry Your Cross Like a Hero*. This is a book I would recommend to anyone. She has several points in there that I have never thought of before. I have signed up for her emails and one I received on May 18, 2016, talked about praise. She explained that many battles are won with song and that we don't have to be a worship leader to sing praises to God. There is power in praise. She says, "As we wield words of adoration and gratitude-often spoken in songs-heaven is accessed, and an audience in the courts of our Father is granted." She goes on to say, "When we sing, God is magnified. His dominion is declared over our situation. So when we choose to praise Him in the midst of battles unseen, He fights for us." An army cry, 2 Chronicles 20:21, won a battle.

> - After consulting the people, Jehoshaphat appointed men to sing to the Lord and to praise him for the splendor of his[a] holiness as they went out at the head of the army, saying: "Give thanks to the Lord, for his love endures forever." (2 Chronicles 20:21, NIV)

That is power! We need to use this mighty weapon of praise to see our battles won. But we have to open our mouths and praise Him.

Praise may mean something different to different people. Singing, giving thanks, reminding God of His promises, or praise that comes from your spirit and soul, are all wonderful ways to praise God. For more, see the section entitled praise.

Now that we have seen some of our weapons for our battles, we need to remember to stand strong in them. Learn more about each one of them on your own and get them down into your hearts. This helps you use them to the best of your ability. We saw what Paul said about standing firm earlier in Ephesians 6, but Jesus also gave us a promise we can look forward to.

> - You will be hated by everyone because of me, but the one who stands firm to the end will be saved. (Matthew 10:22, NIV)

Jesus also promised, in John, that if we would abide in His Word then we would be set free. That is a great promise when you are in a battle.

> - So Jesus was saying to the Jews who had believed Him, "If you abide in My word [continually obeying My teachings and living in accordance with them,] you are truly My disciples. And

OK, GOD, LET'S START FROM HERE

you will know the truth [regarding salvation], and the truth will set you free [from the penalty of sin]." (John 8:31–32, AMP)

Journal entries from Him include the following:

- This battle is raging, but you win in the end with Me at your side.

- Fight spiritually with My Word and come to know Me better. Learn more about Me so you can use more of Me. Take Me with you on purpose and trust Me to fight your battles while you learn.

I was a little confused at one point because we hear it both ways. (1) Let God fight your battles. (2) Put your armor on and stand firm against the enemy. When I asked Him about this, this was His comment:

- I fight in the higher Spiritual realms and you fight in your own spiritual ways. You do what you can and I will do the rest.

We realize we all have battles to fight and we all need God to help us in our time of need. He has given us weapons to help, such as battle armor and the use of prayer and praise. When I find myself in a battle, I gear up and say, "OK, God, let's start from here."

Chapter 9

PHYSICAL AND SPIRITUAL PAIN

"Aren't you tired of being sick and tired?" I had heard that many times before, but it had not manifested in my life yet. I definitely was sick and tired, but my body had not caught up with my spirit and understanding. And, the understanding was very shaky, too. I had heard many different teachings and well-meaning, but inaccurate comments from people.

"God has healed you, but you must believe enough. You don't have enough faith to believe that He can heal you."

"You haven't really received His healing because you don't want it bad enough." And the total kicker was, "You just want the attention. You are not really sick at all!" Wow, did I want to hit that last set of people. They were mainly doctors and were surprised to find out there really was something wrong with me.

So I have had a checkered past with illnesses of many kinds. Most of it has taken place over the last twenty years. However, when I realized the truth of God's Word, and began to use it in my life, I saw major changes.

OK, GOD, LET'S START FROM HERE

The truth is that Jesus took our sicknesses on the cross over two thousand years ago. That was it. He did it and it was taken care of from that day on. He has done everything He will ever do in that area. Everything that comes against us today is covered under what He did for all of us. Every pain, every hurt; it's a done deal. The only problem holding me back was that I did not realize the power He had given me with this precious gift.

I was a Bible-believing Christian. I was saved at the age of 6, and I have had a close walk with the Lord ever since then. Some times were closer than others, of course, but I always knew that Jesus loved me and that by His stripes I was healed.

- But he was pierced for our transgressions, he was crushed for our iniquities; the punishment that brought us peace was on him, and by his wounds we are healed. (Isaiah 53:5, NIV)

- "He himself bore our sins" in his body on the cross, so that we might die to sins and live for righteousness; "by his wounds you have been healed." (1 Peter 2:24, NIV)

I knew these scriptures; I repeated them over and over. And I was healed of many illnesses. The only thing was that I didn't realize the power I had in those words. I was given the authority to use those words and make them real in my body. I "knew" them in my mind, but I had to "know" them in my heart.

These verses are true and when you believe in them, you will see results. The only thing is, God works on His timetable. We may not see manifestations right away, but we certainly should. Our bodies are under the control of our authority and that comes from the Holy Spirit. When we speak the lies our body is telling us, such as pain, it has to obey what we say. (See the section of Authority in this book.)

God wants us well. He has already healed us, and He wants us walking in that healing. He has done everything He ever can do, so begging Him to heal us is something that He can't do at this point. He has already done it, and He can't do it again. He doesn't need to!

I keep journals of the words God speaks to me, but they are not just meant for me. These words are meant for everyone. Here is an entry He spoke about this subject.

> ~ You have all the Authority. I cannot heal you anymore. You have to take your healing and expect the manifestation to come. Never give up. My timing is perfect.

Many people, believers even, will say that you have to have enough faith in God in order for Him to heal us. But that would mean that we have to do something to earn His healings, and that is not what the Bible says. As we see in the first two scriptures, we are and have been healed. Period.

I am not saying that we should stop praying. Prayer is a powerful, effective way to receive our healing. It says in James 5:16 that prayer is powerful.

- Therefore, confess your sins to each other and pray for each other so that you may be healed. The prayer of a righteous person is powerful and effective. (James 5:16, NIV)

I'm reminded of the scriptures in Daniel 9–10 of when the Angel of the Lord came to visit him. He was praying, and the Angel came right away in chapter 9, but in chapter 10, the angel was delayed three weeks due to evil forces.

God hears your prayers and answers them right away, but sometimes our miracles or manifestations are delayed. That does not mean that we stop believing or give up due to lack of physical signs of healing. We may be healed by His stripes, but sometimes it takes our bodies time to catch up.

Many times in the New Testament there are signs of the healings that Jesus performed. He had to have the faith of the people

He healed, rather by them or loved ones, because they did not have the power that we have today. Jesus had not died yet, so they only had the power to believe in what He could do, by the Holy Spirit flowing and working in Him. In all the Gospels, the first four books of the New Testament, we find many times Jesus healed the sick and oppressed. Here are a few examples.

- The centurion replied, "Lord, I do not deserve to have you come under my roof. But just say the word, and my servant will be healed. (Matthew 8:8, NIV)

- She said to herself, "If I only touch his cloak, I will be healed." Jesus turned and saw her. "Take heart, daughter," he said, "your faith has healed you." And the woman was healed at that moment. (Matthew 9:21–22, NIV)

These people had the faith in Jesus to heal them. Now, we have the faith that He has already healed us by the power of His Name. When we realize the authority He has given us through the Holy Spirit in His Name, we can believe for anything in His will; especially healings, since we know it is His perfect will that we are healed.

- For this reason I am telling you, whatever things you ask for in prayer [in accordance with God's will], believe [with confident trust] that you have received them, and they will be *given* to you. (Mark 11:24, AMP)

But it wasn't just until the New Covenant that God healed people. Certainly not! There are several places in the Old Testament that God healed. In Psalms there are many times that people, especially David, cried out for healing and received it.

- But as for me, afflicted and in pain— may your salvation, God, protect me. (Psalm 69:29, NIV)

- Lord my God, I called to you for help, and you healed me. (Psalm 30:2, NIV)

Jeremiah also knew about the absolute healing of God. These people knew God would heal them because He loved them.

- Heal me, Lord, and I will be healed; save me and I will be saved, for you are the one I praise. (Jeremiah 17:14, NIV)

We see from this that we need to keep our eyes on God and not on our circumstances. In the journals I have, God has spoken many words meant for all people. Please understand these words are meant for you personally.

- Remember, physical pain and trouble are fleeting. Keep your eyes on Me.

- You don't have to figure everything out all at once. Your body is very intricate and you have many things happening in your life. Your body can only take so much and you are pushing it to the limits. Relax and rest in Me.

We know that we can rest and relax in God and His love. Psalms 91 lets us know all about this. The whole chapter is wonderful, but we can see these truths in the first two verses.

- Whoever dwells in the shelter of the Most High will rest in the shadow of the Almighty.[a] I will say of the Lord, "He is my refuge and my fortress, my God, in whom I trust." (Psalm 91:1–2, NIV)

We don't need to be upset or pushing ourselves too far, trying to do things on our own. That doesn't work very well, and we can end up doing more damage than good. He talks about this.

- It hurts Me to see you hurting and stressed out. You need to rest and relax in Me. You are trying too hard to do everything on your own. Don't take Me out of the equation when you are walking out My Will. Yes, you have to walk, but only in My strength. You won't get anywhere good on your own. Don't take everything on your shoulders. You may be walking, but I am here with you. I am fighting the battles and leading the way. Just because you have to do your part doesn't mean I stop doing Mine! You need to trust Me to lead you and allow Me to fight the battles with you. Some of them for you. You walk in My peace and strength.

- I love you and it hurts Me to see you hurting when I am right here with My arms opened wide, ready for you to run into them.

There is another side to the pain that we feel. Our bodies are not only the problems we have when we are in pain. There are Spiritual battles we have to face, too. These battles can manifest in the way of physical problems. Here are some things He says in the journals.

- The body is flesh and weak, but the Spirit is life and strength.

We find two scriptures that talk about this subject. This is what Jesus said to His disciples the night before He was killed. He knew how our bodies work.

- "Watch and pray so that you will not fall into temptation. The spirit is willing, but the flesh is weak." (Matthew 26:41 and Mark 14:38)

- Physical mortal bodies will wear out, but you will never wear out if you keep your Spirit alive and keep your Joy!

- I love you and you must treat your body right. It wears down because it is of this world, but when this happens your Spirit should take over. Don't give into your feelings. Let your Spirit tell you how you are. Trust your Spirit. It will never let you down when you put Me in control and walk by and in the Spirit. Trust me. I have designed you this way. Body down, Spirit up! Trust Me and come soar with Me.

- Your body is decaying and of this world, but your Spirit should never feel pain.

He gives us some encouragement by showing us examples of how our physical bodies and Spirits have to balance each other out.

- It doesn't matter if there is something wrong physically, you must balance it out spiritually. Make your God (Me) bigger than your circumstances. Little physical strength—large spiritual strength.

- Don't let your physical body take precedence over your spiritual one.

- Your body is under attack, but you are letting your Spirit be under attack, too. That is how satan works. If he can just make you focus on one thing to get your eyes off of Me, he will do anything.

OK, GOD, LET'S START FROM HERE

If you are like me, there may be many times when you are physically hurting, but the doctors can find nothing wrong. Sometimes that is because you are in a spiritual battle that affects our physical bodies. He explains it this way:

- There is nothing this world will find wrong with your body when it is spiritual warfare.

- You have to rest physically and spiritually fight.

There were several realizations I came to during the time of writing these journals, and I want to share them with you. Remember, these are truths I realized through Him, so they are my words and not His.

1. It is not how much I believe that makes You heal me. You have already healed me, and I just have to walk in that.
2. It's so hard to tell sometimes if there is an assault to my body or to my Spirit.
3. Pain must bow to You since you conquered it and You are in me.

God reminds us that we cannot do any of this without Him. We can't truly function and walk with Him if we don't put Him in control and allow Him to lead and guide us. That is why He sent the Holy Spirit. The Spirit leads us and guides us into all truth.

- But when he, the Spirit of truth, comes, he will guide you into all the truth. He will not speak on his own; he will speak only what he hears, and he will tell you what is yet to come. (John 16:13, NIV)

In the journal, He talks about the subject of the impossible coming true. Matthew and Mark also record the account of Jesus speaking on this subject.

- You cannot do this on your own; it's not possible. But with Me—All things are possible. Take heart—I have overcome the world and that means your physical problems too.

- Jesus looked at them and said, "With man this is impossible, but with God all things are possible." (Matthew 19:26, NIV)

- Jesus looked at them and said, "With man this is impossible, but not with God; all things are possible with God." (Mark 10:27, NIV)

As He said in the journal, we can take heart because He has overcome the world. Jesus says this in John 16:33.

- "I have told you these things, so that in me you may have peace. In this world you will have trouble. But take heart! I have overcome the world." (John 16:33, NIV)

God also says this in a journal entry and in the Bible:

- Manifestation will come, but until then, just trust and believe—then you will receive.

- Hearing this, Jesus said to Jairus, "Don't be afraid; just believe, and she will be healed." (Luke 8:50, NLT)

He says of healings:

- Results are only testimonies to Me.

Our results of healings should be shared with others. Other people are blessed and we realize how great God is when we recount how far we have come, and how we have been used by God. This puts hope into everyone. The hearer is given hope for their affliction, and we receive hope that we can have the strength to win another battle when it comes our way.

I want to reiterate that I cannot know all the diseases that you may be battling right now. I do not know when your manifestations will come, but I know that whatever you are facing, God did not give it to you. He is a good God who can only give good gifts. He does not cause illnesses or sickness of any kind. The only answer I have for you is to trust in God; pray, thanking God for the healing He has already provided; take your authority; and believe it will be done. He has done it, so receive that truth and put it into practice in your life. He will work everything out for good as it says in Romans 8:28.

- And we know [with great confidence] that God [who is deeply concerned about us] causes all things to work together [as a plan] for good for those who love God, to those who are called according to His plan *and* purpose. (Romans 8:28, AMP)

Revelation promises us that we, who have accepted Him as our Lord and Savior, will eventually have glorified bodies with no pain or problems.

- And God shall wipe away all tears from their eyes; and there shall be no more death, neither sorrow, nor crying, neither shall there be any more pain: for the former things are passed away. (Revelation 21:4, KJV)

So when I have a pain in my physical body, I stand on my authority in the Name of Jesus and rebuke it in my body. When it is Spiritual, I call on the Name of Jesus and trust that He will guide me.

Sometimes I forget to do these things right away, and He lovingly reminds me. Then, all I can do is give everything up to Him and say, "OK, God, let's start from here."

Chapter 10

RELATIONSHIP

God wants a personal relationship with each and every one of us. That is what He wants most. He wants our love and He wants our thanks but all that is included in our relationship with Him. It is all about our relationship with God. I cannot stress that enough. Without a relationship with Him we don't have much of anything. Yes, believers will go to Heaven, but it won't be the same there as it will be when we have a close and personal relationship here on earth. He reiterates this in a journal entry that He spoke to me for you. He speaks these words to you personally.

> ~ Life is very precious and fleeting. It is only a small blip in time. That's why you need to reach people and tell them the truth—the whole truth. The truth is that those believers are going to Heaven, but it's all about the relationship. They can have a better relationship with Me here on earth and thus in Heaven. If they get to Heaven and don't know much about Me, it won't be the same. They need to know now, to understand then.

He wants us to not just accept Him as our Lord and Savior and then stop there. He wants us to grow and learn more about Him, because that is where our joy comes from. He wants us to have fun here on earth. He created everything with His words and He lovingly gave us all we have. We need to not only be thankful but come to know Him better by enjoying the life He gave us.

Maybe you have not had a great life on this earth, but when you put your whole trust in Him, He can make the changes in your life that need to be made. He loves you more than you will ever know. Jesus died on the cross for you and He would have done it if it were just for you alone. He loves you and cannot stand to not have a relationship with you. He describes it this way:

- It all boils down to Me and My relationships. I want a strong relationship with ALL My children. So many are lost and confused. They don't really know what to believe. Bring it back to Me.

We find in Jeremiah 29 that God knows the plans He has for us. He wants to prosper us, and we can have that by having a relationship with Him.

- For I know the plans I have for you," declares the Lord, "plans to prosper you and not to harm you, plans to give you hope and a future. Then you will call on me and come and pray to me, and I will listen to you. [13] You will seek me and find me when you seek me with all your heart. (Jeremiah 29:11–13, NIV)

He wants us to seek Him so we can have close relations with Him. He loves us and is ready for us, but we are the ones who have to come to Him. We have to let go of ourselves and run into His open arms. We need to trust and show Him that we want a relationship too.

There are many kinds of relationships with God. We can just believe in Him, or know about him, but not really know Him. We can acknowledge Him only when we have time, or we can have the best relationship by spending time with Him and inviting Him into our everyday lives. He wants to be part of every decision we make and every thought we have.

In a right relationship with Him, we know Him so well that we can only get our true love and joy through Him. We see this in 2 John.

- Love means doing what God has commanded us, and he has commanded us to love one another, just as you heard from the beginning. (2 John 6, NLT)

- Anyone who wanders away from this teaching has no relationship with God. But anyone who remains in the teaching of Christ has a relationship with both the Father and the Son. (2 John 9, NLT)

One way we know we have a relationship with God is by showing others how to have their own relationship with Him. We are to be disciples of Christ and show our love and affection to others. We need to let others know this very important information. We see this in the letter Paul wrote to the Colossians.

- For God wanted them to know that the riches and glory of Christ are for you Gentiles, too. And this is the secret: Christ lives in you. This gives you assurance of sharing his glory. So we tell others about Christ, warning everyone and teaching everyone with all the wisdom God has given us. We want to present them to God, perfect[a] in their relationship to Christ. (Colossians 1:27–28, NLT)

He talks about this in the journal.

> ~ You need to have a child-like trust. It hurts Me to see so many children abused and hurt, but give everyone an opportunity to have a relationship with Me. People are hurting. Reach out your hands and snatch them out of their path of destruction. They may not see it but they are headed the wrong way and you can help them.

Jesus also showed us some examples of wrong relationships in the Bible. He teaches about a man who hoarded money and loved it more than God. Luke shows us the outcome of this.

- "But God said to him, 'You fool! You will die this very night. Then who will get everything you worked for?' "Yes, a person is a fool to store up earthly wealth but not have a rich relationship with God." (Luke 12:20–21, NLT)

We also see an example of a rich young man. Jesus told him the way to have a right relationship with Him was to sell all he had and give it to the poor, for he had let money rule his life.

- But when the young man heard this, he left grieving *and* distressed, for he owned much property *and* had many possessions [which he treasured more than his relationship with God]. (Matthew 19:22, AMP)

The Lord shows us, in the very first commandment, how He longs for a relationship with us.

- You must worship no other gods, for the LORD, whose very name is Jealous, is a God who is jealous about his relationship with you. (Exodus 34:14, NLT)

Since Jesus died for our relationship, we now see how we can have a great relationship with Him. He explains that He is our Good Shepherd and we are His sheep. Sheep follow their shepherd because they know his voice. We are to be that way with Jesus. We are to have such a close relationship with Him that we know what he says to us all the time.

- The gatekeeper opens the gate for him, and the sheep recognize his voice and come to him. He calls his own sheep by name and leads them out. ⁴ After he has gathered his own flock, he walks ahead of them, and they follow him because they know his voice. (John 10:3–4, NLT)

In the journal He says this about His sheep.

- I want happy, thankful sheep that want to be with Me.

We need to want to have God in our lives and be open to a wonderful, close relationship with Him. We have to initiate because He is always ready for an intimate relationship with us.

Believers are also known as the bride of Christ. We are His beloved and He wants us as His own.

- For I am jealous for you with the jealousy of God himself. I promised you as a pure bride to one husband—Christ. (2 Corinthians 11:2)

It's just like a groom waiting expectantly for His bride. He is excited to have a relationship with her. He longs for her just as Christ longs for us. It is not with a physical expectancy but a spiritual one. He longs to be one with our spirits. That is why He sent the Holy

Spirit to us, so that we could have a true relationship with God. We see this in the words spoken by Him in the journal.

> ~ I don't want a begrudging bride. I want a joyful, expectant bride. I want her to be smiling and happy, not caught off guard. I don't want converts, I want relationships.

We can have that wonderful relationship with God when we come to the end of ourselves and realize we cannot live the right way in this world without Him. We have to ask Jesus to be our Lord and Savior. We need the Holy Spirit to have this relationship. If you have not done either of these, then you can find how to do that out at the back of this book.

It is important to have that relationship with God, because we need Him to navigate this life and He longs to bless us. He gets joy in blessing us, but He can only bless us so much until we have that amazing relationship with Him. When we give ourselves wholly to Him then He can move in a real way in our lives. Invite Him in and ask Him how you can have a closer relationship with Him. He loves to tell you how you can better your walk with Him. Ask and you shall receive more understanding of His love.

Sometimes I start to lose my sight and let distractions come in between us. In those times I turn to Him and say, "OK, God, let's start from here."

Chapter 11

PRAISE

Praise may mean something different to everyone. Some people may hear the word praise and think only of singing. That is definitely one way to praise God, but there are other ways. Thanksgiving is a big way of praising God. Another way is to remember of all the things God has done in the past, not only in the Bible, but in your life also. This really is for our benefit. It builds up our faith. When we take our eyes off of our circumstances and look only to God, we can't help but praise Him. Our Spirit and soul are made to praise God. God made us in His image, and that is love and praise. He even praises us for the things we do because He loves us so much.

As mentioned previously, one way God speaks to me is through a journal. I write what He says and it is meant for not only me, but for everyone. These words are from Him to you.

- Put everything else aside and just focus on Me. That is part of Praise.

- Your soul and spirit long to praise Me. When you let go and just focus on Me, praise automatically comes out.

OK, GOD, LET'S START FROM HERE

The dictionary definition of praise includes such things as

- the act of expressing approval or admiration or commendation.

- the offering of grateful homage in words or song, as an act of worship.

Praise is something we do. We are doing it with our spirits, but sometimes we have to think about saying it out loud. As mentioned in the definition, it is expressing such things as admiration. We praise people we look up to. Unfortunately, some people get praised for doing things unpleasing to God. On the other hand, some people really do deserve our praise when they do God's will. We just have to remember that all people are only human and we are supposed to praise God more than people.

- Praise Me for Who I AM, not what I can do for you.

The definition also has commendation in it. When our loved ones do something great we praise them with our words. Praise to God can be just words spoken from our lips to His ears. We lift His Name high and give Him the honor He deserves. Praise Him as the King of Kings and Lord of Lords. There is nothing good that cannot be said about God Most High.

In the journal, I had a moment where I took the time to just praise God. These words can be said to Him at any time, and I wanted you to have a guideline if you were unsure where to start. These are my words to Him.

- (Me) You are the Alpha and Omega—the Beginning and the End. You are the all in all. I love You and magnify You and glorify You. Please don't ever let me take for granted that I am speaking to the God of the Universe. And don't let me ever forget that You are my Abba Father—my Daddy.

You may praise Him in all kinds of ways, but just praise Him from your heart. It doesn't matter what words you use, just lift His Name on high and give Him all the glory and respect He is due.

Here are some examples of praises being said from the people in the Bible. Psalms has wonderful examples of people praising God for who He is.

- I cried out to him with my mouth; his praise was on my tongue. (Psalm 66:17, NIV)

- My mouth is filled with your praise, declaring your splendor all day long. (Psalm 71:8, NIV)

As mentioned, praise is not only done in song, but that is a *great* way to please God. Singing praise as an act of worship is a wonderful way to usher in or enter into God's Presence. He loves to inhabit the praises of His people. Songs are powerful emotionally. They can make us happy, sad, and everything in between. God feels elation when we stop our own little world and look only to Him. He is honored to have us put Him before everything and just tell Him that we love Him.

- Sing to him, sing praise to him; tell of all his wonderful acts. (1 Chronicles 16:9, NIV)

Psalms is a great place to start when learning more about praising God. A definition of psalm is: a sacred song or hymn. There are many verses in Psalms guiding us in ways to praise Him. I encourage you to look some up for yourself.

In the New Testament, we find Paul and Silas in the midst of a trial, and they have an interesting, awesome way of dealing with it. They praised their way out. They were in jail, not just the county jail, but the innermost dungeon! It was bad. But they knew God was good and that He had only their best interest at heart. So they began singing and praising Him. It says the whole prison could hear them. In the middle of the praises their chains just fell off. The really cool thing, though, is that they didn't jump up and run out. They were so caught up with praising God that it didn't matter where they were. Many good things came from those praises, as is often the case. So when in the middle of a trial, praise is always an answer! (Acts 16:25–31).

A journal entry from God reveals how He feels about hearing our praise.

> ~ I love you and long to hear the praises of My people.

Thanking God is part of praise too. Thanking Him in songs was very powerful back in the Bible and was used as a weapon in war. We see in 2 Chronicles that even then they knew how strong singing praises with thanksgiving to God was.

- After consulting the people, Jehoshaphat appointed men to sing to the LORD and to praise him for the splendor of his holiness as they went out at the head of the army, saying: "Give thanks to the LORD, for his love endures forever." (2 Chronicles 20:21, NIV)

Once, when the people praised Him in His temple, they found out how powerful praising Him could really be.

- In unison when the trumpeters and singers were to make themselves heard with one voice praising and thanking the Lord, and when they raised their voices accompanied by the trumpets and cymbals and [other] instruments of music, and when they praised the Lord, *saying*, "For *He* is good, for His mercy *and* loving kindness endure forever," then the house of the Lord was filled with a cloud, so that the priests could not remain standing to minister because of the cloud; for the glory *and* brilliance of the Lord filled the house of God. (2 Chronicles 5:13–14, AMP)

When we look to Him and thank Him for all He has done, we are showing Him how grateful we are. God has done so much and given up all He holds dear because He loves us. You feel good when someone else thanks you for something you did. It feels good to be recognized for your hard work, and God is the same way. He gets happy and enjoys His children and He loves to hear that we care for Him and appreciate all He has done for us.

Thanking God is not something that can only be done in song. Thanking Him can be done with just spoken words, too. Here are a few verses on thanksgiving that prove this point.

- Now, our God, we give you thanks, and praise your glorious name. (1 Chronicles 29:13, NIV)

- [*Psalm 106*] Praise the LORD. Give thanks to the LORD, for he is good; his love endures forever. (Psalm 106:1, NIV)

Another aspect of praise is reminding God of His precious promises. This is not for God's benefit. He knows all that He has promised us, but it is great for us. We find many promises in the Bible, but this can include things He has spoken into your specific life, too. Gentiles are grafted into the divine promises that God gave to the Israelites. He fulfilled all those promises with Jesus, so that we now may obtain all the gifts God promised them. You can easily search out some by reading your Bible, or searching verses on websites. We have many resources today to help us find out more about our precious Heavenly Father. When we remind ourselves of these promises, it boosts our confidence and puts joy and hope in our hearts. We need to keep those hopes and truths in front of us all the time to remember who we are and what we have in Him.

We have special feelings when we praise God. We find hope, joy and an earnestness in our hearts. Here are some good examples of these things.

Hope

- But as for me, I will wait *and* hope continually, And will praise You yet more and more. (Psalm 71:14, AMP)

Joy

- The Lord is my strength and my [impenetrable] shield; My heart trusts [with unwavering confidence] in Him, and I am helped; Therefore my heart greatly rejoices, And with my song I shall thank Him *and* praise Him. (Psalm 28:7, AMP)

Heart

- I will give thanks *and* praise You, O Lord my God, with all my heart; And will glorify Your name forevermore. (Psalm 86:12, AMP)

Salvation is the main reason we praise God. He lovingly gave Jesus and we should all praise Him for that. Jesus died on that cross for everyone; believers and unbelievers. It says in Romans that we were still sinners when Christ died for us.

- But God clearly shows *and* proves His own love for us, by the fact that while we were still sinners, Christ died for us. (Romans 5:8, AMP)

We have the wonderful gift of salvation when we do believe and ask Him into our lives, but He still died that day even for people who will never believe in Him. That is how much He loves us. He gave His ultimate gift so that we might have His righteousness. Jesus gave us His life so we could have eternal life with Him. That is something to praise Him for!

Here are some verses of people showing their praise to God on the subject of salvation.

- Heal me, Lord, and I will be healed; save me and I will be saved, for you are the one I praise. (Jeremiah 17:14, NIV)

- Praise be to the God and Father of our Lord Jesus Christ! In his great mercy he has given us new birth into a living hope through the resurrection of Jesus Christ from the dead. (1 Peter 1:3, NIV)

- Sing to the Lord, praise his name; proclaim his salvation day after day. (Psalm 96:2, NIV)

In the book of Psalms, we find a great example for praising God.

- Praise the Lord.[a] Praise God in his sanctuary; praise him in his mighty heavens. Praise him for his acts of power; praise him for his surpassing greatness. Praise him with the sounding of the trumpet, praise him with the harp and lyre, praise him with timbrel and dancing, praise him with the strings and pipe, praise him with the clash of cymbals, praise him with resounding cymbals. Let everything that has breath praise the Lord. (Psalm 150, NIV)

In a journal entry, He states clearly what we need to do for Him. He knows we will be blessed when we just do this.

~ Keep praising Me.

Praise can be singing our love or just talking to God. There is no wrong way to praise God. If it comes from your heart, that is all that matters. Just open your heart and mouth and let your spirit praise God. He loves you and wants to be acknowledged, thanked and loved by us.

It's wonderful to know that our praises will not end on this earth, and that all of Heaven right now is praising God along with us. The angels, among others, are worshiping God saying blessings, like this one found in Revelation, all the time.

- Saying, "Amen! Blessing and glory *and* majesty and wisdom and thanksgiving and honor and power and might belong to our God forever and ever. Amen." (Revelation 7:12, AMP)

Sometimes I find myself complaining to God about my trivial situation when I should be praising Him for all He has already done for me. When you start to praise Him, everything else falls to the side. Your problems become smaller the larger you make God in your life. Praising God takes your eyes off you and puts them on Him. Then not only is He blessed, we are too.

When I realize I am only complaining to God and not really giving my attention to Him, it only makes my problem worse. Then I start to praise Him, and I give my situation over to Him. I praise Him and say the words He loves to hear, "OK, God, let's start from here."

Chapter 12

THANKS

Thanksgiving is not only a time we, as Americans, stop and remember what our forefathers did when they came to this country. It's not supposed to be just one day you pause and recognize God and what He has done for you. Thanksgiving is an attitude. It's a part of you. It is the way you see things in life.

There are different kinds of people in this world. Some see the good in everything. They are often known as optimists. These people are usually thankful for all they have. We, as believers, need to be like this. We need to be giving thanks to God always. Even in hard times we need to rejoice and give our thanks and praise because He is always working on our behalf to bring out the best in us.

There are also people who do not give thanks to God. They are often very miserable people. They don't feel things are ever going their way. They feel that the world is against them. They do not know the love and grace of Jesus Christ.

There are many verses in the Bible that talk about thanksgiving and how we can give it. The most popular verse on thanksgiving is repeated over ten times in the Old Testament. The first one we see is in 1 Chronicles.

- Give thanks to the Lord, for he is good; his love endures forever. (1 Chronicles 16:34, NIV)

There are many other times this truth is echoed throughout the Bible; 2 Chronicles and Psalms the other books with this exact phrase.

We find several ways of thanking God in the Bible. We find in Psalms a great way to thank him is through singing.

- I will give thanks to the Lord because of his righteousness; I will sing the praises of the name of the Lord Most High. (Psalm 7:17, NIV)

- I will praise God's name in song and glorify him with thanksgiving. (Psalm 69:30, NIV)

- Let us come to him with thanksgiving. Let us sing psalms of praise to him. (Psalm 95:2, NLT)

Some of these verses may be found in the Praise section of this book, but they are so good and such a reminder of how we ought to not only praise God, but thank Him too. In fact, there are a few verses about praise that include thanksgiving also.

- Enter his gates with thanksgiving and his courts with praise; give thanks to him and praise his name. (Psalm 100:4, NIV)

David had a real sense of how to give praise and thanksgiving to God. He was a man after God's own heart as we see below:

- After removing Saul, he made David their king. God testified concerning him: "I have found David son of Jesse, a man after my own heart; he will do everything I want him to do." (Acts 13:22, NIV)

David said a prayer after everyone gave money towards the building of the temple in Jerusalem. David thanked the Lord for Who He was and all that He had done, as evident in this part of the prayer.

- Now, our God, we give you thanks, and praise your glorious name. (1 Chronicles 29:13, NIV)

Psalm 9 has continuous mention of thanksgiving, praise and singing, as many Psalms do. I encourage you to read and find some for yourself. We can all learn several things from reading these encouraging words while learning the sorrow of the author as well. They often remind God of their pain, but in the same Psalm thank Him and praise Him, for they know He will not forsake those who love and trust Him.

As mentioned before, thankfulness is an attitude. When I write in my journals, and God answers me, He gives me words for everyone. These words are meant for you. He says,

- Thankfulness is a very important attitude. It shows you trust things will or have come to pass, and that you receive it with open arms.

When we do thank God, we need to do so out of joy. Your heart and spirit will flow with joy and gladness when you look to Him and begin to realize how awesome He really is. Joy is a wonderful, healing thing that we must possess to get through this crazy thing called life. You can learn more on this concept in the Joy section of this book.

There is joy in thanksgiving. There are several scriptures in the New Testament where Paul speaks of joy, reminding the readers of the joy they have through Jesus.

- Being strengthened with all power according to his glorious might so that you may have great endurance and patience, and giving joyful thanks to the Father, who has qualified you[a] to share in the inheritance of his holy people in the kingdom of light. (Colossians 1:11–12, NIV)

- Rejoice in the Lord always. I will say it again: Rejoice! Let your gentleness be evident to all. The Lord is near. Do not be anxious about anything, but in every situation, by prayer and petition, with thanksgiving, present your requests to God. And the peace of God, which transcends all understanding, will guard your hearts and your minds in Christ Jesus. (Philippians 4:4–7, NIV)

- Rejoice always, pray continually, give thanks in all circumstances; for this is God's will for you in Christ Jesus. (1 Thessalonians 5:16–18, NIV)

These last two verses talk about prayer also. Prayer is another way of thanking God. When you get with Him and pray, you need to remember to thank Him for all He has done. Taking time to stop and pray shows God you are thankful enough to spend time with Him and trust He will hear you. Trust is discussed further in the Trust section of this book.

In 1 Timothy, we see that prayer is linked to God's Word.

- For everything God created is good, and nothing is to be rejected if it is received with thanksgiving, because it is consecrated by the word of God and prayer. (1 Timothy 4:4–5, NIV)

God is honored by our thanksgiving. He has this to say in the journal about how proud He is and how we honor Him when we thank Him.

~ You make Me so proud when you thank Me.

- You always thank Me for your successes. Keep doing that because as the Word says: every good and perfect gift is from above! (James 1:17). So thank Me and praise Me for it. I love that. It honors me and I am very much a God of honor. You see it all over My Word, especially in the Old Covenant. Not everything changed with the New Covenant. I kept My Word and made it better for everyone. But it still happened on My honor. You honor those you love and appreciate. That's why I said, "Honor your Father and Mother . . ." I am your Father and I am to be honored. I love you and you loving Me brings Me great honor.

God says this concerning joy and thanksgiving in the journal:

- I love your thankful heart. Never lose that and never lose your joy. The two go hand-in-hand. When you are thankful, you are joyful, and when you are joyful—truly joyful—you are thankful.

Paul encourages the believers to be thankful to and for Christ. He says this many times. He tells about the victory we have in Christ. Here are a few verses that show his love and understanding of what Jesus was really about.

- [*Thanksgiving*] I always thank my God for you because of his grace given you in Christ Jesus. (1 Corinthians 1:4, NIV)

- The sting of death is sin, and the power of sin is the law. But thanks be to God! He gives us the victory through our Lord Jesus Christ. (1 Corinthians 15:56–57, NIV)

- It is written: "I believed; therefore I have spoken." Since we have that same spirit of[b] faith, we also believe and therefore speak, because we know that the one who raised the Lord Jesus from the dead will also raise us with Jesus and present us with you to himself. All this is for your benefit, so that the grace that is reaching more and more people may cause thanksgiving to overflow to the glory of God. (2 Corinthians 4:13–15, NIV)

- And whatever you do, whether in word or deed, do it all in the name of the Lord Jesus, giving thanks to God the Father through him. (Colossians 3:17, NIV)

Jesus knew how important it was to give thanks to the Father for everything. Every time he broke bread, He prayed a prayer of thanksgiving as we see in the following verses.

- And he directed the people to sit down on the grass. Taking the five loaves and the two fish and looking up to heaven, he gave thanks and broke the loaves. Then he gave them to the disciples, and the disciples gave them to the people. (Matthew 14:19, NIV)

- Then he took the seven loaves and the fish, and when he had given thanks, he broke them and gave them to the disciples, and they in turn to the people. (Matthew 15:36, NIV)

Jesus also did this privately with His disciples on the night before His death. He told them to do this in remembrance of Him. He did these things so we would always remember to do this with Him in mind. But the first thing He did was give thanks.

- While they were eating, Jesus took bread, and when he had given thanks, he broke it and gave it to his disciples, saying, "Take and eat; this is my body." (Matthew 26:26, NIV)

- Then he took a cup, and when he had given thanks, he gave it to them, saying, "Drink from it, all of you. (Matthew 26:27, NIV)

The disciples didn't understand what Jesus was talking about, but we do since we know what Jesus did for us. Now, before every meal, we should give thanks to God for the food He has provided, because Jesus showed us this example.

Sometimes I get overwhelmed when I think of all the things I have to be thankful for like, salvation, forgiveness, discipline, love, joy and everything else. I realize I have so much to be thankful for, and I can never say all the things I can feel. I asked Him about this one night and I told Him that since I can't come up with all the words I want to, I would just say, "Thank you!" This was His reply to me and you if you are feeling this way.

- I know you—every single part of you. When you thank Me it is from your heart. You may not be thinking of everything you are thanking Me for, but your heart does. It knows it all and it thanks Me for every single thing when you say, "Thank you!"

When we thank God we are acknowledging Him for all He has done for us. We are giving Him the credit for helping us through our situations. We need to thank Him for our everyday lives too. In everything we do we need to give credit to God. We need to realize that He is working on our behalf all the time. He talks about this in the journal.

- Thank you for giving Me credit for helping you through your day. There is a lot that I do that goes unnoticed by everyone.

We find a verse in a Psalm that is repeated four times, and when God repeats Himself, we need to listen and take notice. It is found in Psalm 107.

- Let them give thanks to the Lord for his unfailing love and his wonderful deeds for mankind. (Psalm 107:8,15,21,31, NIV)

Thanksgiving is a huge part of our walk with the Lord. We are to be thankful for everything, knowing that God has only the best for us. When things look bleak, we can rest assured that God turns what satan means for evil into a blessing. God only has the best for us. He loves us and longs to hear our praises and thanks for all He has done. It brings Him honor and us joy. Be thankful always and everything will turn out for your benefit. Then, we can turn to Him wholeheartedly and say, "Thank You, Jesus!"

I find myself in valleys sometimes and my life looks bleak, but then I remember that God is in control. He has my life in His hands when I yield to Him. I look back and thank Him for all He has done. Then I thank Him for all He is doing, and by the time I have done that, I find Myself joyful. I say the words that lift my soul, "OK, God, let's start from here."

Chapter 13

JOY

"Happy, happy, joy, joy" is something I often say to myself to perk me up when I am feeling on the down side. It's funny because it started out as something I made myself say, most of the time with gritted teeth. I hated saying it at times, but I didn't realize the power of words. Now I know that when I say that, I start to feel it. I think about the joy that is about to flood my life and I usually start smiling or laughing.

Joy is not just a feeling; it's a way of being. We can have joy on the worst days of our lives because it is not just "happiness." Pure joy comes from the love of God. When you have God on the inside, you have joy. It's there. Whether you acknowledge it or not is up to you. You have the power within you to have a great day or a terrible day.

Your attitude decides the outcome of your feelings. You can choose to have a good attitude and let your joy flow from within, or you can choose to have a negative attitude and not only have a bad day, but you can probably lead others into one too. The point is you get to choose.

In the Bible we find the word joy is mentioned over 240 times. God loves you and He wants you to be joyful! He mentions this point time and time again in the journals that He speaks to me through.

These words are meant for everyone. When you see the word "you" please read it as if it straight from His heart to yours. Here are a few entries.

- Keep your joy. That is what he (satan) wants the most of all. He has no joy, so he comes to steal yours. He thinks if he has yours it will make him happy. It makes him feel better to take your joy, but it doesn't last. He loses it and then he comes to take it again. It is a cycle.

- Rejoice for Me as I rejoice for you.

- You fill Me with Joy and Gladness. You make My heart smile.

- Don't let satan try to steal the thing I died to give you—Joy! There is Joy in Salvation. There is Joy in healing. There is Joy in Me.

It may seem hard to believe, but the Bible tells us that Jesus went to the cross out of joy.

- We do this by keeping our eyes on Jesus, the champion who initiates and perfects our faith. Because of the joy awaiting him, he endured the cross, disregarding its shame. Now he is seated in the place of honor beside God's throne. (Hebrews 12:2, NLT)

Physically, He may not have been joyful, but I believe He was thinking of us on that cross and rejoicing that we would be able to have a relationship with Him when it was all over.

We have strength through our joy. One of my favorite verses in the Bible is

- Nehemiah said, "Go and enjoy choice food and sweet drinks, and send some to those who have nothing prepared. This day is holy to our Lord. Do not grieve, for the joy of the Lord is your strength." (Nehemiah 8:10, NLT)

This verse has helped me through countless situations. I also like to pair it with:

- I can do all things through Christ which strengtheneth me. (Philippians 4:13, KJV)

If I can do *all* things through Christ, then I can do it joyfully! I don't need to suffer through struggles and begrudgingly work my way through trials. Paul mentions this when he spoke to the Romans about how we as believers are to be.

- Never lagging behind in diligence; aglow in the Spirit, *enthusiastically* serving the Lord; [12] *constantly* rejoicing in hope [because of our confidence in Christ], steadfast *and* patient in distress, devoted to prayer [continually seeking wisdom, guidance, and strength] (Romans 12:11–12, AMP)

James also speaks of trouble and how we are to respond to it.

- Consider it nothing but joy, my [a]brothers and sisters, whenever you fall into various trials. Be assured that the testing of your faith [through experience] produces endurance [leading to spiritual maturity, and inner peace]. (James 1:2–3, AMP)

Joy is not always our first thought when things go wrong, but if we are joyful, things have a way of working out for good. That is how God works; He takes bad and uses it for good. He is a good God and can only do good things. He never hurts us or sends evil things for us to endure. We have to go through trials, but it is how we act in the midst of them that show our true colors. That's when joy needs to kick in the most.

Here are some more uplifting words He has said in the journals.

- Keep your Joy always. Keep searching and finding.

- I give you strength through My Joy! Keep your joy and rest.

- My joy is your strength. Your joy keeps My joy coming.

I said to God in one of my journals on this topic, "You make me joyful in times of despair. You make this life worth living." He is the only thing that is worth it. There is nothing else that really keeps us going. That is why people of this world have no true joy; they do not have the loving, joyful God in their lives. He does warn us at times to not give into despair and just give up.

- It's hard at times to keep your joy, but don't let laziness creep in and keep you stagnant.

Joy is contagious. It flows from you to others. When my son gets upset or frustrated with me, I just stare at him and smile. He tries his hardest not to look at me, but I just keep it up or make a funny face, and he will end up smiling almost every time. I will teasingly say, "Don't smile! Don't do it!" If you can get your focus off of what is upsetting you, then you can count on your joy to take over and let the positive shine through.

The next time you find yourself in a negative situation, stop and purposefully say out loud, if possible, "I am not going to let satan steal my joy!" Then, smile. Smile a real smile. You may have to wing it at first, but eventually your spirit will take over and you can't help it. It depends on your faith and how you let God flow in your life. He wants to be the one you call on for your joy.

One way people in the Bible showed their joy was in praise. Many times it came with singing. When you open your mouth and let songs come forth from your heart, it blesses not only Him, but you also. Your spirit is built up and it just fills you with love. It is shown in many different Psalms that singing abounded. These scriptures are just a few. Read these and just let them soak into your spirit.

- The Lord is my strength and my shield; my heart trusts in him, and he helps me. My heart leaps for joy, and with my song I praise him. (Psalm 28:7, NIV)

- Sing joyfully to the Lord, you righteous; it is fitting for the upright to praise him. (Psalm 33:1, NIV)

- But let all who take refuge in you be glad; let them ever sing for joy. Spread your protection over them, that those who love your name may rejoice in you. (Psalm 5:11, NIV)

- The whole earth is filled with awe at your wonders; where morning dawns, where evening fades, you call forth songs of joy. (Psalm 65:8, NIV)

- Satisfy us in the morning with your unfailing love, that we may sing for joy and be glad all our days. (Psalm 90:14, NIV)

God showed this in one of the journal entries. It's interesting to know that we can make Him joyful too. While we are singing over Him, He is singing over us!

- You make Me sing for joy. When you praise, not only do you feel better, I feel amazing!

We also find along with singing, shouts can come out of our mouths, too. In 1 Kings, we find that singing and shouting caused the earth to shake.

- And all the people followed Solomon into Jerusalem, playing flutes and shouting for joy. The celebration was so joyous and noisy that the earth shook with the sound. (1 Kings 1:40, NIV)

- My lips will shout for joy when I sing praise to you—I whom you have delivered. (Psalm 71:23, NIV)

- Shout for joy to the Lord, all the earth. Worship the Lord with gladness; come before him with joyful songs. Know that the Lord is God. It is he who made us, and we are his[a]; we are his people, the sheep of his pasture. (Psalm 100:1–3, NIV)

- Shout for joy to God, all the earth! (Psalm 66:1, NIV)

This last one is one of my favorite. All creation loves the Lord and knows Who their Creator is. They know God and they bow to Him in worship. Everything living grows on His Word. The universe is held together by the words of His lips. He spoke the world into existence (Genesis 1:1). He created everything that is found in nature. Even Jesus said this in reply to His disciples being silent.

- He replied, "If they kept quiet, the stones along the road would burst into cheers!" (Luke 19:40, NLT)

Even the rocks know who Jesus is and even the mountains will bow down to Him. So if they can shout out to their creator, shouldn't we do so even more, since He is our loving Heavenly Father, and we are made in His image?

We also can be filled with joy in His presence. When He is with us, joy will always abound, even if we don't "feel" joyful at the time. We just realize what He has done for us and given as a free gift.

- Surely you have granted him unending blessings and made him glad with the joy of your presence. (Psalm 21:6, NIV)

- You make known to me the path of life; you will fill me with joy in your presence, with eternal pleasures at your right hand. (Psalm 16:11, NIV)

Joy comes through the Holy Spirit. When we are saved, we receive the seal, or promise, of the Holy Spirit. When we realize that we need to ask Him to move in our lives, by being baptized in the Holy Spirit, we receive perfect joy. He is the power of God released in us. That is the where the power of all the promises Jesus left us comes from. All the power and signs and wonders Jesus had, came from the Holy Spirit within Him. Jesus was definitely joyful! There are scriptures that point to this very subject.

- And the disciples were filled with joy and with the Holy Spirit. (Acts 13:52, NIV)

- For the kingdom of God is not a matter of eating and drinking, but of righteousness, peace and joy in the Holy Spirit. (Romans 14:17, NIV)

- You became imitators of us and of the Lord, for you welcomed the message in the midst of severe suffering with the joy given by the Holy Spirit. (1 Thessalonians 1:6, NIV)

- I pray that God, the source of hope, will fill you completely with joy and peace because you trust in him. Then you will overflow with confident hope through the power of the Holy Spirit. (Romans 15:13, NLT)

When you are joyful, thanksgiving flows. When you are focused on God, you can't help but be joyful in your spirit. When you are joyful, thanksgiving for all you have spills from your spirit. God has this to say from the journals.

- Keep that joy, for that is where thanksgiving flows from.

- I love your thankful heart. Never lose that and never lose your joy. The two go hand-in-hand. When you are thankful, you are joyful, and when you are joyful—truly joyful—you are thankful.

So when we are thankful, we can open our hearts and let our joy flow through the Holy Spirit residing in us. We release that joy in different ways, including praise by singing, and just talking to Him. Getting our eyes off of ourselves and onto Him, we can't help but become joyful! He loves us and He is full of not only joy but fun too. He reiterates to me all the time that He is a *fun* God. He loves to see us happy and having fun. That is one of the reasons I think laughter is the best medicine.

- A cheerful heart is good medicine, but a crushed spirit dries up the bones. (Proverbs 17:22, NIV)

There are physical benefits to laughter. It releases endorphins in our brains; the body's natural feel-good chemicals. Endorphins promote an overall sense of well-being and can even temporarily relieve pain. Laughter decreases stress hormones and increases immune cells and infection-fighting antibodies, thus improving your resistance to disease. (www.helpguide.org/articles/emotional.../laughter-is-the-best-medicine.html)

God wants us healthy and joyful! He created us in His image, and we are to be joyful people who love to laugh and have fun in Him. God is not a rigid Supreme Being who only looks down on His people and makes them worship Him. In fact, the very opposite is true. He loves us so much He allows us to choose to love Him. He loves to hear from us and be included in our lives. He wants to see us joyful and having fun in Him, because that is how He made us. His fun is not the "fun" of this world, but it is true unadulterated fun. To learn more, read the section of Fun in this book.

When we choose to love God and invite Him into our lives, we not only receive salvation, but all of the fruits of the Spirit, found in Galatians 5:22–23. He wants us joyful and happy. No matter what situation we find ourselves in, we can always look to Him and rejoice.

When I find myself starting to feel down or unhappy I take a hold of myself, release a smile, and say, "OK, God, let's start from here."

Chapter 14

GIFTS/GIVE

Giving something away has a boomerang effect. When you give, you get. This is true with good and negative things. The Bible tells us plainly that you reap what you sow.

- Do not be deceived: God cannot be mocked. A man reaps what he sows. (Galatians 6:7, NIV)

When you give blessings, you get blessings. Not only from people on this earth, but from God.

- The Lord gives strength to his people; the Lord blesses his people with peace. (Psalm 29:11, NIV)

- Lord Almighty, blessed is the one who trusts in you. (Psalm 84:12, NIV)

When you say negative things to others, you are cursing them, and cursing yourself. You receive the negative you give.
He says this in my journal for everyone to accept:

> ~ Give life to another and you get life in return. Give love, get love. Give peace, get peace. Grow people, grow yourself.

When you speak life into someone else, then you are receiving life from your Loving Heavenly Father. You are loosening your power of life from the authority given you, by Jesus, through the Holy Spirit, to speak life and not death. If you do not know Jesus and His authority or the Holy Spirit, you can do that with the prayers in the back of this book. The truths in this book will make much more sense to you then.

We find in Proverbs:

- Death and life are in the power of the tongue: and they that love it shall eat the fruit thereof. (Proverbs 18:21, KJV)

You do not have to be a believer to have power in your words. You can give life and kill with a little member of your body—the tongue. It may not even be something you are doing on purpose, but you are affecting other people's lives. I find this especially true in my life with my son. I have been entrusted by God to take care of him and I need to speak life over him. Positive words receive positive results. Kids are very susceptible to the things their parents say to them. You can change their lives forever by what you speak over them. That is a big responsibility, so we need to watch what we say.

Our words not only affect other people they also have a definite result in our lives. We can affect our future by what we say. If we say negative things about ourselves then we will reap what we say. It's not a complicated idea, but it is hard to do, if we have to retrain our minds. It may take a while to change but it is worth the effort.

So when we give good gifts, the Father recognizes that. He loves to give us good gifts in return. He says this in the journal:

> ~ I give good and precious gifts to My children. I love blessing My children. It makes Me happy to

please others. I just want them to be happy and please Me in return. I want them to be thankful and grateful for everything they have because it all came from Me.

- You are My good and perfect gift.

We are not only gifts to Him, but we are to be gifts to the world. When He gave the Great Commission, to the disciples, in the end of Matthew, He gave them His power; everything in Heaven and earth.

- Jesus came up and said to them, "All authority (all power of absolute rule) in heaven and on earth has been given to Me. Go therefore and make disciples of all the nations [help the people to learn of Me, believe in Me, and obey My words], baptizing them in the name of the Father and of the Son and of the Holy Spirit, teaching them to observe everything that I have commanded you; and lo, I am with you always [remaining with you perpetually—regardless of circumstance, and on every occasion], even to the end of the age." (Matthew 28:18–20, AMP)

He says it this way in the journal:

- I have given you everything in Heaven and on earth and under the earth.

He gave us the authority He had so we could go do the work we were created for, furthering His Kingdom. But don't ever think that furthering His Kingdom is boring work. He loves us and longs to give us the desires of our hearts when they are in the right place. This is what He says:

~ I want to give you everything your heart desires. Just make sure it desires what will further My Kingdom.

We saw earlier that He loves to give good gifts to His children. Those gifts include blessings in all areas of our lives. God wants you to prosper in every way. You do not need to be a poor, unhappy, or unsuccessful believer. He wants to bless you physically, financially, and spiritually; every part of your life. We are to be joyful, thankful people. When we are happy, He is happy.

He not only wants us to prosper but to thrive! He will turn our sorrows into joy. The disciples were working hard to bring the Gospel (the Good News) to the people everywhere. This is how Paul explains part of their situations.

- Our hearts ache, but we always have joy. We are poor, but we give spiritual riches to others. We own nothing, and yet we have everything. (2 Corinthians 6:10, NLT)

That is how it was back then and how it is sometimes today. We as disciples need to put other's needs ahead of our own, but when we do, we receive many blessings back. He explains that though they may not have had worldly riches, they had joy, and that is a blessing in itself.

God says in the journal that we are to give Him our worries and He will give us the blessings we need. That sounds like a great deal to me!

~ Give Me your thoughts and worries and I will clothe you with righteousness.

He only wants the best for us. That is His desire. And only He knows how to give it to us. Even though we may not see our blessings right away, we have them none the less. This is how He puts it:

OK, GOD, LET'S START FROM HERE

> ~ Wait patiently for Me. I only want the best for you and I know how to give it to you.

He gives us several commands with a promise in James.

- Submit yourselves, then, to God. Resist the devil, and he will flee from you. ⁸ Come near to God and he will come near to you . . . (James 4:7–8, NIV)

The beginning of verse 8 is a special promise for us. In the journal He explains it this way:

> ~ Freely give as I have freely given. Come close to Me and I will come close to you. Look, it says you have to do your part first. You must initiate. You have to do, to get things done. Do unto Me as you would do unto others.

God wants us to give Him our all. We need to empty ourselves and fill our hearts and lives with Him. Many people say they are an empty vessel, meaning they are emptying themselves preparing for Him, but I say I am an overflowing vessel because I am ready and willing to do His will. I am not empty at all. I am full of Him.

God expects no less of us. We are His children and He deserves not only our love, but our willingness too. We need to push ourselves out of our comfort zone and go live life, on purpose, for Him. That is when the blessings start to flow. And I think it is important to mention that you may not see your blessing right away, but they are coming, so don't give up. You may never see the harvest from the seeds you have sown, but you will when you get to Heaven. There will be special blessings there that you will definitely receive and enjoy. So don't give up blessing others when you don't receive yours right away. You are even more blessed when you have to wait because the blessings are bigger. Never give up hope and joy. Speak life.

God reminds us of this in an entry:

- Push yourself to the limit with Me. Don't give Me less than what you can give. Take and eat. This is My body broken for you. I gave you *all* of me and I want *all* of you in return.

He reminded me of this. It was for me personally but we can all take the important part away from it.

- Give Me away. Don't hide Me in this book (my journal).

I believe that thanking God for all he has done is very important. It is a blessing to Him and a blessing to us.

We were doing a series on the Fruits of the Spirit on our internet radio show, The Messengers, so these were in my heart. We find the Fruits of the Spirit in Galatians 5:22–23.

- But the fruit of the Spirit is love, joy, peace, forbearance (patience), kindness, goodness, faithfulness, gentleness and self-control. Against such things there is no law. (Galatians 5:22–23, NIV)

I told God in one of my entries: Thank You for blessing Me with All the Fruits of the Spirit! You give each of those to me so that I can give them to others.

Those are blessings that God has given to us and they are to be shared with people everywhere. Here are some we find in Psalms. This is the King James Version, so we may not be used to the language, but just listen to the spirit of what it is saying.

- Bless the LORD, O my soul: and all that is within me, bless his holy name. Bless the LORD, O my soul, and forget not all his benefits: Who forgiveth all thine iniquities; who healeth all thy diseases; Who redeemeth thy life from destruction; who crowneth thee with lovingkindness and tender mercies; Who satisfieth thy mouth with good things; so that thy youth is renewed like the eagle's. The LORD executeth righteousness and judgment for all that are oppressed. (Psalm 103:1–6, KJV)

Now go out and speak life and bless others. Give and you will get. You reap what you sow. Sow life, receive life. Freely give as He has freely given.

When I hear negative words coming out of my mouth, I stop and not only apologize, but change my thinking and change my speech. I open my mouth and let these words come from my heart. "OK, God, let's start from here."

Chapter 15

FUN

So many times when people think of God they think of a staunch being somewhere in the sky that only wants us to live a perfect life. And they imagine Him rolling His eyes when we can't. Let me tell you, that is not God! That is not at all what Jesus died for and not the Loving Father that we all need to worship.

Too many times, religion has crept in and only taught us the God of the Old Testament—the One who had to "smite" people, bring death, and punishment. That was never His intent. He only had to do those things when the people He loved would not listen to Him and were destroying themselves. He loved all those people, but was bound by rules He had put into place after Adam and Eve ate from the tree of the Knowledge of Good and Evil in the Garden.

God's intention was for the wonderful relationship He had with Adam and Eve. He made us all in His own image. He loves every one of His creations; even the ones who don't believe in Him. It breaks His heart, but He still loves them. God intended to have friendship and relationship with His creations, His children. He has always only wanted to be our friend and loved one.

When satan tempted Adam and Eve beyond restraint God had to set new rules and laws for people. They had, unknowingly, given their authority over all the earth into the hands of satan. God had to restrain satan from killing all the people.

God had many close friends and people He was close to in the beginning, such as Abel, who longed to please Him (Genesis 4). God never left Adam and Eve behind. He still loved them and blessed them. He didn't love them any less for making the wrong decision. He just had to change His way of communication. There were people, like Enoch, who were so close to God that he was just taken into the air to be with Him (Genesis 5:24). Abraham was called a "Friend of God" (James 2:23). I think God had fun with all these people. The one thing they had in common was that they loved God and wanted a relationship with Him. That is all God wanted too.

The people He had to correct, sometimes even to the point of death, were leading His loved ones astray. They were sort of "messing up His plans" you could say. He had to choose the greater good over the evil in those people's hearts. He had to stop the bad so the good could flourish.

God could not talk to everyone one-on-one back then. He had to use interpreters such as the Prophets. They were special people who listened to what God was telling them. Then they relayed the messages to the others. God also gave some people visions and dreams. Certain ones were able to interpret those dreams, such as Joseph and Daniel for example. You can find their stories in Genesis (starting in 37) and the book of Daniel. These are only a few examples and I encourage you to find more for yourself.

In order to make amends with God, for the people's sins, there had to be a blood offering and animals were used for this. The people took their very best animals and brought them to the priests to be made right with God. It was hard, I imagine, but when they did it with a cheerful heart, they were able to receive blessings from God.

And then, along came Jesus! Jesus was everything that was good and right. By sending His own Son, God made everything right with

His people again. Jesus was the spotless lamb that became that blood covenant once and for all on that cross. Now, when we accept Jesus into our hearts and put Him as our Savior, we can communicate with God on the same level as Adam and Eve, before the fall. He talks to us and we can commune back with Him. We are free to be close to Him again, this time, without the interpreters.

So can we have fun with God? Absolutely! He is a fun God! He had fun with people all throughout the Bible. We see even in the Old Testament:

- So I recommend having fun, because there is nothing better for people in this world than to eat, drink, and enjoy life. That way they will experience some happiness along with all the hard work God gives them under the sun. (Ecclesiastes 8:15, NLT)

God is a fun God, who incidentally created fun! He says to us in one of my journals:

- You know I am a FUN God. I love to have fun. I invented it! I love to laugh. I love to smile and always do when I think of My children. I may be a mystery to you, but you are not a mystery to Me. I know all of you, and I love you all (wholly).

- I am a fun God. The old God who had to enforce the law is now released, by the blood of Jesus, to have a fun relationship with you. I still had fun back then. Abraham and I had fun. I had fun with the other people, too, the ones who would listen. But now I am free to let loose and be in you every day.

Many people assume that fun is from the devil, and the world's fun certainly is. But real fun is relaxing in God and doing the things of His will. When you give yourself over to God completely, things will become easier and you can enjoy your life. God has created all the things of this earth for our enjoyment. He created life and He wants us to enjoy ours, not by the world's standards, but by His.

- Go *your way*, eat your bread with joy and drink your wine with a cheerful heart [if you are righteous, wise, and in the hands of God]; for God has already approved *and* accepted your works. (Ecclesiastes 9:7, AMP)

The devil is a liar. He can only take things God has given and twist them into evil. He has no new tricks up his sleeve. He can only lie. When we are not strong enough in God and His Word, satan can come in and lie to us about the things we worry about most. When we stand strong and realize the authority we have in the Name of Jesus, we can put him in his place, which is under our feet. (See Authority section) He only has the power that we give him. He has done this with the fun God intended us to have. He has taken our true Godly fun and twisted it into lies about what fun really is. The people who seem to be having fun in this world are all usually very miserable, sad, and lonely. Now, that is not what God intended!

I am convinced God loves to smile! He created us to be cheerful. He mentions this subject many times throughout the Bible. Here we see some in Proverbs.

- A cheerful heart is good medicine, but a broken spirit saps a person's strength. (Proverbs 17:22, KJV)

- A heart full of joy *and* goodness makes a cheerful face, But when a heart is full of sadness the spirit is crushed. (Proverbs 15:13, AMP)

- A cheerful look brings joy to the heart; good news makes for good health. (Proverbs 15:30, NLT)

If you have spent much time in church, you are probably familiar with this next verse, but I think it can be used in other ways than the money that most people refer it to.

- Let each one give [thoughtfully and with purpose] just as he has decided in his heart, not grudgingly or under compulsion, for God loves a cheerful giver [and delights in the one whose heart is in his gift]. (2 Corinthians 9:7, AMP)

I do believe in giving my tithes and offerings with a cheerful heart, but I think we could use this verse with other things, such as giving love to one another or blessing someone. There are many ways to take this verse if you stop and truly study it. I challenge you to find out what it really means to you.

God loves a cheerful giver and a cheerful spirit. We are made to love the things of God. We have been given a wonderful blessing of being able to be close to God. He is only words away. He loves you and longs to hear from you. He is ready to listen when you are ready to talk. Search your heart and give it completely to Him. In return you will receive peace and joy. Remember God is a *fun* God. Enjoy Him as He enjoys you. This is a quote from Him in the journal.

- Enjoy this life while you can. It may be a crazy world you live in, but live it with Me and unto Me and we will have so much fun.

I love this one. I actually love them all, but I am a very joyful person. So when I feel my joy slipping away, I gather myself together and say, "OK, God, let's start from here."

Chapter 16

GOODNESS

Goodness is found within, not by works or deeds. Many people go around trying to be perfect or trying to prove themselves by their actions. There are many people out there who do great works and help with the less fortunate, but as God says in His Word:

- And though I bestow all my goods to feed the poor, and though I give my body to be burned, and have not charity (love), it profiteth me nothing. (1 Corinthians 13:3, KJV)

If people do good things, but they must make a show about it, they are not really full of the goodness of God. They can do good things but if it doesn't come from the heart, they get no blessings from the Lord. Actions will not get you to Heaven. Only salvation does.

God described it this way in the journal:

~ Goodness is Who I Am and what I show to everyone. Goodness is My heart.

Psalms shows us that we ought to praise the Lord for all he has done for us.

- Oh that men would praise the Lord for his goodness, and for his wonderful works to the children of men! (Psalm 107:15, KJV)

God went on to say in the journal:

~ In order to have true goodness, you must have a repentant heart and care for others.

Scripture shows us an example of this.

- Or despisest thou the riches of his goodness and forbearance and longsuffering; not knowing that the goodness of God leadeth thee to repentance? (Romans 2:4, KJV)

Goodness is not just something you do. When it is genuine, it is part of who you are. It's who we were made to be. We were made to be so much more than we are right now. We were made to be loving, gracious, and overflowing with goodness. The fruits of the Spirit, found in Galatians 5:22–23, show us more of the wonderful things God gives to us. Then we can give it to others.

- But the fruit of the Spirit is love, joy, peace, forbearance (patience), kindness, goodness, faithfulness, gentleness and self-control. Against such things there is no law. (Galatians 5:22–23, NIV)

God says it this way:

~ Goodness comes from the heart. It is something you show because it is part of you. Goodness seeps out of your very being when it comes from Me.

OK, GOD, LET'S START FROM HERE

We are made to show good acts to others out of the goodness in our hearts. Not out of the goodness of our wallets or flashy extravagant luxury. We can give good gifts but they need to be from our hearts. God says it again here:

> ~ There are "good" people out there who know how to do "good" things, but true goodness is found in people with My heart. People can *act* good but they cannot *be* good without Me.

There are differences between doing good acts and doing acts of goodness. It is never wrong to give when you are prompted to. It is never bad to give good gifts. It is only wrong to give good gifts when you expect something in return. Here is what God told me about the differences.

> ~ And there is a difference between doing a good act [actions] and showing the goodness of your heart. If people see "goodness" without the other gifts [of the Spirit] then they are seeing only actions or outward appearances. They are not measuring goodness the way I do. I see goodness in the thoughts and gifts that come from the heart; a broken and contrite heart that centers on Me.

Scripture shows us how Paul felt about this issue when talking to the Thessalonians.

> • With this in mind, we constantly pray for you, that our God may make you worthy of his calling, and that by his power he may bring to fruition your every desire for goodness and your every deed prompted by faith. (2 Thessalonians 1:11, NIV)

God again reiterates:

- People can do good things, but without goodness in their hearts, it matters nothing.

God shows us examples of how to extend goodness to others. He has graciously given to us, so we know how to graciously give to others. The book of Psalms has several scriptures concerning this.

- Answer me, Lord, out of the goodness of your love; in your great mercy turn to me. (Psalm 69:16, NIV)

- But you, Sovereign Lord, help me for your name's sake; out of the goodness of your love, deliver me. (Psalm 109:21, NIV)

These verses show us that goodness flows out of God's heart; the way it should flow out of our hearts. When we have His heart we can't help but have goodness spilling out.

Psalms also brings up another point about goodness. Psalm 116:12 asks,

- What shall I return to the Lord for all his goodness to me? (Psalm 116:12, NIV)

Then, it goes on to answer that very question in these verses.

- They celebrate your abundant goodness and joyfully sing of your righteousness. (Psalm 145:7, NIV)

- Oh that men would praise the LORD for his goodness, and for his wonderful works to the children of men! (Psalm 107:15, KJV)

OK, GOD, LET'S START FROM HERE

Praise and joyful singing bring about God's goodness and it brings out the best in everyone. When you praise God it raises your spirits and lifts your joy. Then goodness not only flows from God, but from your heart also.

He also reminds the Romans that good deeds are not the most important things. It says,

- For the Kingdom of God is not a matter of what we eat or drink, but of living a life of goodness and peace and joy in the Holy Spirit. (Romans 14:17, NLT)

When our hearts are full of goodness we can hardly contain it. Every good and perfect gift comes down from the Father of lights (James 1:17). When we receive the goodness of God we release it in ourselves. When we overflow with that goodness it spills over into the lives of everyone we are around. Many people today say, "Pay it forward." That means they have received a free gift from someone and they pay for someone else to have a free gift. That is goodness but it is only true goodness when it comes from the heart. Some people do that because they believe it is "good karma" and they are expecting something in return. That is not God's goodness. He loves us and gives us good gifts with no expectations.

- A good man brings good things out of the good stored up in his heart, and an evil man brings evil things out of the evil stored up in his heart. For the mouth speaks what the heart is full of. (Luke 6:45, NIV)

I think the best way to sum it all up is with the scripture in Palms 23. The whole chapter is wonderful, but we find in verse six how it mentions God's goodness.

- The LORD is my Shepherd [to feed, to guide and to shield me], I shall not want. He lets me lie down in green pastures; He leads me beside the still and quiet waters. He refreshes and restores my soul (life); He leads me in the paths of righteousness for His name's sake. Even though I walk through the [sunless] valley of the shadow of death, I fear no evil, for You are with me; Your rod [to protect] and Your staff [to guide], they comfort and console me. You prepare a table before me in the presence of my enemies. You have anointed and refreshed my head with oil; My cup overflows. Surely goodness and mercy and unfailing love shall follow me all the days of my life, And I shall dwell forever [throughout all my days] in the house and in the presence of the Lord. (Psalm 23, AMP)

I love to show God's goodness to others, but when I find myself not giving with a right heart, I correct my mistakes by asking for forgiveness. Then I say, "OK, God, let's start from here."

Chapter 17

DREAMS AND GOALS

Dreams: we all need to have them. I'm not talking about the things you think about at night during your sleep, although they may certainly come from that. I am talking about the dreams you have for your life. Not only the big picture dreams, but also the goals you set for yourself every day.

Maybe you have dreams of being married, living in a certain house, or driving a favorite car. Dreams can be big or little. The only thing you have to do is listen to the dreams God gives you. You may be dreaming something for your life that God does not want you to have. In that case, anything you try to do to reach those dreams is not going to be successful. If it is not what God wants, then it usually is what satan wants, so be careful whose dreams you are really following.

God wants you to dream big. He wants you to open your mind up to unlimited possibilities from Him. He has special plans for your life. He wants to give you the desires of your heart, but they have to line up with His Word. He loves you and longs to bless you. In my journal He says this:

~ Be sure to dream My goals.

～ Ask Me out loud for the desires of your heart. We both need to hear them. Keep your dreams in front of you always. Keep your dreams alive and Dream Big. I AM a Big God who loves to have fun and I have lots of fun blessing you and enjoying your Praise and Worship. I love it when you talk to Me, no matter where or when. I love hearing you and being included in your day.

God wants you to have everyday dreams and goals. Goals start out small and then grow. In order to get to a big dream, you must make small goals. One step at a time is how you get anywhere. You cannot get to the end without going through the middle.

In Terri Savelle Foy's ministry, she has a teaching called, "Mind over Mattress." In it she remarks how many successful people start their day out with good morning rituals. These small, everyday habits can lead to very large dreams coming to fruition. Every successful person has started out with a dream. That doesn't mean that all your dreams will be successful to the outside world. But when your dream is realized it will be very successful and satisfying to you.

What is your dream? Where do you want to be in five, ten, twenty years? How do you want your life to be? These are all questions I want you to stop and take a minute to really think about.

Where do you see your life going?

Are you on the right road?

Is God part of these dreams?

Have you asked Him where He wants you to be in the future? Ask Him. He loves to reveal Himself to you.

God wants you to dream big but tangible. There is no point in dreaming of being someone or something you are not. You will never be able to be someone else, but you could be more than you ever expected if you let God rule your dreams. He is the God of the Universe and He wants to see you succeed more than you do! He loves you and wants to bless you. When you are living for God your dreams can become realities.

Terri Savelle Foy encourages what she calls vision boards. In her book, *Dream it. Pin it. Live it.*, written and published by Terri Savelle Foy Ministries, she explains this concept more clearly. In essence, these boards are tangible places you put ideas of your dreams on so you can see your goals. For example, if you want a different house, put a picture of that house or just any house to serve as an example. You can write your dreams on paper and put them on the board. It doesn't even have to be a board. It can be any place that will hold something that reminds you of your dreams. If you look at that board, even once a day, you will keep your dreams alive and work toward that goal.

One thing I try to do every day is write my hopes and goals in a notebook. I write what I hope (confidently, joyfully, expect to happen) for this year. This is my second year doing this. I actually got the incentive from Terri Savelle Foy so now I encourage you to do it.

Take something like a notebook and write goals you want to accomplish for the year or any amount of time you wish. Start out the first day by writing everything you can think of. Remember to include God in these decisions! Then, get a new paper the next day and write them all again. Don't look at the first paper; just write your goals from that day. See how many goals you have in common for those days. The ones you really want will come through day after day. Do this for thirty days. When you do something for thirty days, it becomes a habit. I started this habit over two years ago and I still write in it almost every day. It has kept me focused. I love going back in my spiral notebook and seeing all the dreams that have come true. It is very rewarding and I like having my dreams in front of me.

This is the same concept with the dream board. It helps so much to be able to actually look at something and see it with your eyes. When your mind sees it, your heart gets excited! This is what God said in my journal:

~ Make tangible goals that you can see when I answer them. This fuels you forward and brings on more confidence. Start small, then grow.

Remember, every step of faith you take toward your goal will ultimately bring you closer to your dream. He says this:

~ You have to just take a step of faith. Dream Big and then follow Me to the end.

That is very important about following through to the end. Many times we think we want something really bad, but then it takes too much hard work or time, so we give up. Unfortunately, many people have done this with their dreams. They have let their dreams become so big in their eyes that they feel they could never accomplish them. This is due largely in part to not involving God. Their dreams probably could not come true on their own willpower, but with God *all* things are possible. As Jesus says in Mark:

- Jesus looked at them and said, "With man this is impossible, but not with God; all things are possible with God." (Mark 10:27, NIV)

- Jesus said to him, "[You say to Me,] 'If You can?' All things are possible for the one who believes *and* trusts [in Me]!" (Mark 9:23, AMP)

So take those dreams off the shelf or just begin to dream bigger. Ask God what His will for your life is and follow it through to the end. God fueled me on when He said this:

~ When you dream big, big things happen.

This is like a promise. When I feel myself allowing my dreams to fade, I stand up and say, "OK, God, let's start from here."

Chapter 18

LOVE

Love is such a broad subject. We have confused the love of God with the love of this world. We can say, "I love my spouse," and then turn around and in the same breath say, "I love my dog." We can tell our friend we love them and tell God we love Him. So what is the difference? There are all kinds of love, but in order to truly give the love that God gave us, we have to have Him as the Source. He is our example. But we need to make sure we love others with God's kind of love. I'm not saying that it is wrong to love your pet or any of these examples, but we need to put our love in perspective.

God shows His thoughts on this in the journal I keep of His words. These words are for everyone so when you see the word associated with "you" He is speaking directly to you.

> ~ To Me, love is love. To you humans, love is equated with "feelings" from your soul. Mine is equated from the heart and from the Spirit. I love you and that is absolute. You love Me and you may wander and lose faith, but your love is not tied to your feelings. It is tied to your heart. You cannot truly love until you understand that I loved you first. Then you realize true love.

We must realize His true love for us before we can truly love one another. We can love them because God is love and God is with us as believers. But if we don't understand His love, we can only love from our souls. We can "feel" love, but there is no underlying love when we have no foundation to base it on. It is all how our bodies feel and react to the environment around us.

God tells us in His Word, the Bible, how we are to love each other. He said to love each other as ourselves and that is powerful. Jesus said this when asked about the greatest commandment and it was recorded in Matthew 22:36–40, Luke 10:27, and Mark 12:30–31, which we will look at here.

- Love the Lord your God with all your heart and with all your soul and with all your mind and with all your strength.'[a] The second is this: 'Love your neighbor as yourself.'[b] There is no commandment greater than these." (Mark 12:30–31, NIV)

God loves us and there is no better proof of that then we find in John 3:16, (AMP).

- "For God so [greatly] loved *and* dearly prized the world, that He [even] gave His [One and] [a]only begotten Son, so that whoever believes *and* trusts in Him [as Savior] shall not perish, but have eternal life.

The best example, I believe, came from the beginning. God created this world from nothing just for us. He did it all so that we could have life and life with Him. Genesis 1:1 shows us this act of love.

- In the beginning God created the heavens and the earth. (Genesis 1:1, NLT)

In some of the journal entries He explains how He feels.

- I love you and I did all of this- everything- for your benefit.

- I cannot tell you how much I love you, but I can tell you over and over so you never forget.

- I love you. I will say that over and over to you Always! You will never be tired of hearing it and if you are, listen better!

- I love you and only want the Best for My children. I love you and want to see you succeed because when you succeed, I succeed! My Kingdom flourishes when you do My will. You are awesome. You were made to be awesome.

Some people don't know this truth. They just need to realize that God loves them. The way we can tell them is not only by showing them through our lives, but explaining to them what Jesus did for us that day on the cross. He showed us the ultimate act of love when He willfully laid down His life. The Bible says that He even did it with joy. He wanted to do that so that we could have the relationship we are able to have with Him now.

The book of Romans shows us His real love for us.

- But God demonstrates his own love for us in this: While we were still sinners, Christ died for us. (Romans 5:8, NIV)

He says this in the journal.

- Bless My people. They will know you by your love. Just love them. Speak life and life abundantly over them.

- Some people need to be reminded that someone out there still cares for them.

God loves us all alike. He loves the sinner and the believer. He died for all of us. I think He is more excited about the believer but He loves us the same. Here are some things He says about this.

- You can't forget that I love you more than anything else. If you never seek Me or trust me, if you doubt, I will still love you just as much. You can never make Me love you less or more. I love you beyond belief.

- Even if you rejected Me, I would love you no less.

- It's you and Me together always! You know that if you stopped doing everything you are doing now I would love you no less. I love you and I will always love you. Nothing you do or don't do can change that.

We know He loves us, but how do we show our love for Him? Jesus gives us the answer to this question in John.

- "If you [really] love Me, you will keep *and* obey My commandments. (John 14:15, AMP)

He also encourages us from the journal,

- Love Me. Love me more that you think you are capable of.

- Love Me perfectly.

This may seem strange that He asks us to love Him more than we think we can, but He knows we can always go beyond the boundaries we have set for ourselves. Many times we hold back part of ourselves because we are afraid to let go and just let Him take over. But He is the best One to put in charge of us. I encourage you to just let go of your problems and let Him replace them with peace only He can give you. He will flood your life with His perfect love. He also says,

- I love you and I will not let you go astray when you trust Me and put Me in control. Put Me first and leave Me there! I love you and I want to be the One you want.

We also need to get into the Bible and learn from the people who came before us and had great wisdom from God and Jesus himself. He reminds us of this in the journal.

- You are ensconced in the truth of My love and My healing, but you need to be immersed in My Word to be able to learn and grow.

We are not perfect people and we will make mistakes, but that is when He lovingly corrects us. He will not get mad at us and cause problems in our lives. He does not cause strife in our lives because He is a God of love and He only wants the best for us. He will direct us to the right path, and it may seem like a harsh truth, but He will tell us the truth because we need to know we are being disciplined and why. But that does not mean He stops loving us. He tells us these things from the journal.

- This is tough love but it is *love*! I tell you the truth in love but I must tell you the truth.

- I think about you *all* day long and only smile. You can let Me down by not doing what I ask, but I am always thinking good of you and how much I love you. You make My heart smile. I love to be included in your day so please include Me on purpose.

It's important to remember that we are victors with Christ since He loves us so much. We are to be an example to others and they are to know us by our love.

- Yet in all these things we are more than conquerors *and* gain an overwhelming victory through Him who loved us [so much that He died for us]. (Romans 8:37, AMP)

- But those who obey God's word truly show how completely they love him. That is how we know we are living in him. Those who say they live in God should live their lives as Jesus did. (1 John 2:5–6, NLT)

In order to keep God strong in our hearts we need to give Him away. The more we give, the more we get. He loves us so much and we are to love Him too. We can never understand how much He loves us, but we are to live every day loving Him more and offering ourselves up to Him. We can give Him our problems and receive His perfect love in return. Understand that He loves us no matter what we do. He will love us no less when we mess up and we should love Him no less when we go through trials of many kinds.

Here is an entry He gave showing His love for us.

~ You are beautiful, wonderful, perfectly made! I love you, My sweet precious child.

When I let doubt creep in and cause my faith to wane, He reminds me of who I am in Him and I can only say, "OK, God, let's start from here."

Chapter 19

TAKE ME/WANT ME

God is a jealous God. He is jealous for you. He loves you and wants you to be His only. He is also a gentleman and will never go where He is not invited. He loves you so very much, but He will not plant himself in the middle of your life and just take over. You need to give your all up to Him.

If you have loved ones, you understand how nice it feels to be included in their lives. How wonderful do you feel when you are asked to be part of their day? When my teenage son says, "Hey, Mom, you want to play a game?" part of me just melts. He is telling me, in no specific words, that he wants to spend time with me. I love that. He wants to be around me. That makes me feel loved and appreciated.

God is the same way. He loves to be included in our lives. He wants to have a close relationship with us. He wants to be wanted. This is what He says to everyone in my journal:

- Include Me on purpose. I can and will help in every area of your life when you let Me in. Love Me. Just love Me. You know you like to be around people you love and enjoy it even more when they

> ask you to be there. How much more so do you think it is with Me? I love you so much and when you invite Me in and Ask Me My opinion and ask for My help, it is elation!

> ~ I want to be with you all day! I want you to want to be with Me too.

This next entry was said on an ordinary day, when I just asked Him to be with Me. He is saying this to you every time you ask Him to be part of your day.

> ~ I love being with you and included in your day. This may seem like another normal day but it was special to Me just to be with you. You didn't even notice Me all the time, but you did talk to Me often. You asked Me in and I gladly accepted. It feels so good to be wanted by the one you long for.

God longs for you and your attention to Him. He made you specifically just for Himself. He made you to further His Kingdom. In order for you to do that, you must have a right relationship with Him. That includes spending time with Him.

He enjoys every minute, every second, spent with you. One of the journal entries made me stop and think how important He really is. This is what He said,

> ~ Make each day special with Me. Remember Me on purpose. Take Me with you on purpose because you want me there. I know you love Me, but do you like Me enough to want Me around?

This breaks my heart every time I read it because the thought of me not showing God that I want Him included in my life makes me sad. I love Him and I want to show Him that. How do we do that?

We invite Him to be with us everywhere we go. Take Him with you to the grocery store. Take Him with you to work. Take Him with you when you are just driving down the road.

So what does "take Him with you" mean? How do I do that, you ask? Great thing to ask! It is nothing major. There is no specific thing you have to do. You don't need to be on your best behavior and not make any mistakes. All you have to do is say something like, "God, please come with me everywhere I go today. I love you and I invite you into my day."

If you are a believer, you have Jesus on the inside of you already. Because of this, He does go everywhere you go, but you need to ask Him to join you. As I said in the beginning, He is a gentleman and will never intervene in your life without you asking. Just talk to Him. You don't have to do anything special. You just need to show Him how important He is to you by involving Him in your life.

One way of involving Him is to talk to Him. You can say anything you want, whenever you want. He loves it when you just think of Him and speak to Him. This can be done in your head, heart, or out of your mouth. Everyone has different ways they speak to God. You speak to Him in the way that is most comfortable to you. Just acknowledge Him and He will be so excited. He loves you; every part of you.

He says it this way in the journal:

- Take Me everywhere you go. Walk with Me. Talk to Me all the time.

God personally walked and talked to Adam and Eve. He longed to have a relationship with them because He loved them. Guess what? He loves you just as much as He loved them! Even if you are a sinner, which we all are, He loves you. And He wants to have a relationship with you. He is excited to be part of your day no matter if you are a saved believer or not. All you have to do is ask.

"How do I become a believer?" you wonder. It is easy. You say the prayer at the back of this book and mean it with your heart. Your words spoken out loud and a truthful heart will bring you salvation every time. This opens up a right relationship between you and God. Then, you will have more benefits of having Him in your everyday life.

Jesus died for your sins to be forgiven. He already forgave all your sins when His blood was shed on the cross. All is forgiven but you must repent and turn away from your sins. You don't have to be sinless in order to have God in your life. When Jesus came to the earth, He hung out with sinners, as we see in Matthew.

- While Jesus was having dinner at Matthew's house, many tax collectors and sinners came and ate with him and his disciples. (Matthew 9:10, NIV)

And He did so on purpose. He had this to say:

- On hearing this, Jesus said to them, "It is not the healthy who need a doctor, but the sick. I have not come to call the righteous, but sinners." (Mark 2:17, NIV)

He did this because He loved them. He also wanted them to love and accept Him and His Father, God. Your sins are no worse than anyone else's. Sin is sin in God's eyes, but Jesus died for every sin ever committed. All you need to do is ask for forgiveness.

So when you ask God to come in, and be part of your everyday life, He jumps at the chance. He loves you, no matter where you are in your walk with Him. He loves everyone the same. Just release your faith and show God you love Him by including Him in your everyday life.

These are your words from Him, for you:

~ Take Me with you tomorrow on purpose—all day long.

When I realize I have not asked Him to be part of my day, I just take time to ask Him in by saying, "OK, God, let's start from here."

Chapter 20

Positive Affirmations

I was feeling particularly sad one day, so I started thinking of all the things God says I am and all the things He has promised in His Word. Here are some of the things I came up with. I encourage you to repeat these affirmations when you need uplifting. Remember these are words meant for you to speak out loud, not things meant just for me, so when it says "I" it means you.

I have all authority over things in Heaven and earth.

- Then Jesus came to them and said, "All authority in heaven and on earth has been given to me. (Matthew 28:18, NIV)

- I will give you the keys of the kingdom of heaven; whatever you bind on earth will be bound in heaven, and whatever you loose on earth will be loosed in heaven." (Matthew 16:19, NIV)

I have all the power God gave Jesus and more.

- Very truly I tell you, whoever believes in me will do the works I have been doing, and they will do even greater things than these, because I am going to the Father. (John 14:12, NIV)

I have power.

- Counsel and sound judgment are mine; I have insight, I have power. (Proverbs 8:14, NIV)

I have the power to conquer sin and death.

- No, in all these things we are more than conquerors through him who loved us. (Romans 8:37, NIV)

I have joy.
I have strength.

- Nehemiah said, "Go and enjoy choice food and sweet drinks, and send some to those who have nothing prepared. This day is holy to our Lord. Do not grieve, for the joy of the Lord is your strength." (Nehemiah 8:10, NIV)

I have knowledge.

- For in him you have been enriched in every way—with all kinds of speech and with all knowledge—(1 Corinthians 1:5, NIV)

I have love.

- For the Father Himself [tenderly] loves you, because you have loved Me and have believed that I came from the Father. (John 16:27, AMP)

OK, GOD, LET'S START FROM HERE

I have the love of many.

- This is my commandment: Love each other in the same way I have loved you. (John 15:12, NLT)

I have good and precious promises from my Father.

- His divine power has given us everything we need for a godly life through our knowledge of him who called us by his own glory and goodness. Through these he has given us his very great and precious promises, so that through them you may participate in the divine nature, having escaped the corruption in the world caused by evil desires. (2 Peter 1:3–4, NIV)

I have the precious promises of the Holy Spirit.

- But the Advocate, the Holy Spirit, whom the Father will send in my name, will teach you all things and will remind you of everything I have said to you. (John 14:26, NIV)

I have life and life abundantly.

- The thief cometh not, but for to steal, and to kill, and to destroy: I am come that they might have life, and that they might have it more abundantly. (John 10:10, KJV)

I have the power of life and death in my tongue.

- Death and life are in the power of the tongue, And those who love it *and* indulge it will eat its fruit *and* bear the consequences of their words. (Proverbs 18:21, AMP)

I use my words to edify not condemn.

- Let no corrupt communication proceed out of your mouth, but that which is good to the use of edifying, that it may minister grace unto the hearers. (Ephesians 4:29, KJV)

I have a personal relationship with God.

- He made Christ who knew no sin to [judicially] be sin on our behalf, so that in Him we would become the righteousness of God [that is, we would be made acceptable to Him and placed in a right relationship with Him by His gracious loving kindness]. (2 Corinthians 5:21, AMP)

I have You, Lord, and in You I have everything.

- By his divine power, God has given us everything we need for living a godly life. We have received all of this by coming to know him, the one who called us to himself by means of his marvelous glory and excellence. (2 Peter 1:3, NLT)

I have authority over the enemy and darkness.

- They will have the same authority I received from my Father, and I will also give them the morning star! (Revelation 2:28, NLT)

I have the Holy Spirit.

- If you then, though you are evil, know how to give good gifts to your children, how much more will your Father in heaven give the Holy Spirit to those who ask him!" (Luke 11:13, NIV)

OK, GOD, LET'S START FROM HERE

I have the truth.

- Jesus saith unto him, I am the way, the truth, and the life: no man cometh unto the Father, but by me. (John 14:6, KJV)

I have the promise of salvation.

- If you declare with your mouth, "Jesus is Lord," and believe in your heart that God raised him from the dead, you will be saved. For it is with your heart that you believe and are justified, and it is with your mouth that you profess your faith and are saved. (Romans 10:9–10, NIV)

I have the love of my Heavenly Father.

- For God so loved the world that he gave his one and only Son, that whoever believes in him shall not perish but have eternal life. (John 3:16, NIV)

I am an heir with Christ.

- Now if we are children, then we are heirs—heirs of God and co-heirs with Christ, if indeed we share in his sufferings in order that we may also share in his glory. (Romans 8:17, NIV)

I am a child of God.

- Yet to all who did receive him, to those who believed in his name, he gave the right to become children of God— (John 1:12, NIV)

I trust in Christ, therefore I trust in myself.

- Then Christ will make his home in your hearts as you trust in him. Your roots will grow down into God's love and keep you strong. (Ephesians 3:17, NLT)

I know the truth and speak it boldly.
I am as bold as a lion.

- The wicked run away when no one is chasing them, but the godly are as bold as lions. (Proverbs 28:1, NLT)

I am not ashamed of the gospel of Jesus Christ.

- For I am not ashamed of the gospel, because it is the power of God that brings salvation to everyone who believes: first to the Jew, then to the Gentile. (Romans 1:16, NIV)

I am above and not beneath.
I am the head and not the tail.

- The Lord will make you the head, not the tail. If you pay attention to the commands of the Lord your God that I give you this day and carefully follow them, you will always be at the top, never at the bottom. (Deuteronomy 28:13, NIV)

I come behind in no good thing.

- For the Lord God is a sun and shield: the Lord will give grace and glory: no good thing will he withhold from them that walk uprightly. (Psalm 84:11, KJV)

I live, yet not I, but Christ lives in me.

- I have been crucified with Christ and I no longer live, but Christ lives in me. The life I now live in the body, I live by faith in the Son of God, who loved me and gave himself for me. (Galatians 2:20, NIV)

I love everyone He has created.

- "Teacher, which is the greatest commandment in the Law?" Jesus replied: "'Love the Lord your God with all your heart and with all your soul and with all your mind.'[a] This is the first and greatest commandment. 39 And the second is like it: 'Love your neighbor as yourself.' (Matthew 22:36–39, NIV)

I am who God says I am.
I have what God says I have.
I can do what God says I can do, and He tells me I can do ALL things through Him.
I can do all things through Him who strengthens me.

- I can do all this through him who gives me strength. (Philippians 4:13, NIV)

I believe and receive.

- For this reason I am telling you, whatever things you ask for in prayer [in accordance with God's will], believe [with confident trust] that you have received them, and they will be *given* to you. (Mark 11:24, AMP)

I tell others that Jesus is the Way, the Truth, and the Life.

- Jesus told him, "I am the way, the truth, and the life. No one can come to the Father except through me. (John 14:6, NLT)

I will triumph.

- For the sin of this one man, Adam, caused death to rule over many. But even greater is God's wonderful grace and his gift of righteousness, for all who receive it will live in triumph over sin and death through this one man, Jesus Christ. (Romans 5:17, NLT)

I am the victor.
I have the victory.

- For the Lord takes delight in his people; he crowns the humble with victory. (Psalm 149:4, NIV)

I am clothed with righteousness.

- I delight greatly in the Lord; my soul rejoices in my God. For he has clothed me with garments of salvation and arrayed me in a robe of his righteousness, as a bridegroom adorns his head like a priest, and as a bride adorns herself with her jewels. (Isaiah 61:10, NIV)

I put my faith in Him.

- So in Christ Jesus you are all children of God through faith. (Galatians 3:26, NIV)

OK, GOD, LET'S START FROM HERE

I know Jesus is the Son of God.

- Who is it that overcomes the world? Only the one who believes that Jesus is the Son of God. (1 John 5:5, NIV)

I know I will be clothed in glory when I get to Heaven.

- For while we are in this tent, we groan and are burdened, because we do not wish to be unclothed but to be clothed instead with our heavenly dwelling, so that what is mortal may be swallowed up by life. (2 Corinthians 5:4, NIV)

I can hear the words spoken to me by God.
I have an ear to hear what the Spirit is saying.
I have the ear of the Creator of the Universe.
I talk to God and He listens.

- If I had cherished sin in my heart, the Lord would not have listened; but God has surely listened and has heard my prayer. Praise be to God, who has not rejected my prayer or withheld his love from me! (Psalm 66:18-20, NIV)

God tells me what I need to know when I need to know it.
I have the Holy One living on the inside of me.
I love Christ.
I have a kind heart and disposition, but have fierceness in my God.
I am a friend of God.
I know Jesus as my personal Lord and Savior.
I trust in God and all that He has given me.
I have respect.
I believe!

Some of these affirmations you may not believe or have the courage to say about yourself but know that God believes all of them about you. He gives you the opportunity to believe and say these things all the time. They were meant to help me in my time of need, but they can be spoken daily. These are truths from God and His Word. All you need to do is believe and receive.

I pray these help you realize more of who you are in Christ. When I start to forget who I am and what I have, I build myself up by speaking these truths and say, "OK, God, let's start from here."

Prayer for Salvation

The prayer for salvation is the most important one you will ever pray. When you say these words, they will change your life forever when spoken from your heart. You do not have to pray this out loud, but you need to be bold enough to voice your love for God.

In Romans 10:9–10, we see a clear picture of the promise that everyone can be saved and how easy it is to do.

- If you declare with your mouth, "Jesus is Lord," and believe in your heart that God raised him from the dead, you will be saved. For it is with your heart that you believe and are justified, and it is with your mouth that you profess your faith and are saved. (Romans 10:9–10, NIV)

And in Romans 10:13, we see a wonderful promise that no matter who you are or what you have done, you are qualified to accept Jesus.

- For, "Everyone who calls on the name of the Lord will be saved." (Romans 10:13, NIV)

You do not have to speak big lofty words or long, difficult prayers. All you need to do is simply say words from your heart.

Here is an example of a prayer you can repeat out loud.

"Jesus, I believe you died on the cross to save me from my sins. I believe God raised You from the dead. I ask You now to come into my heart and be my Lord and Savior. Please forgive me of my sins. I give my life to You and receive Your salvation now. Thank You, Lord, for saving me. Amen!"

If you just prayed that prayer and meant it with your heart, congratulations, you are a whole new being! You are promised the gift of eternal life with God in Heaven! Your sins are forgiven and your spirit is perfect and as white as snow.

You may feel that you are not saved because nothing around you has changed, but when you said those words, you were changed on the inside. Don't let anyone come and try to tell you that prayer meant nothing, because those small words changed your life forever.

I would encourage you to get a Bible if you don't have one, and if you need one, you may contact me through my website, www.triciadraper.com. You should also find a Bible-believing church and start to get your spirit fed so you can grow in the ways of God.

I also encourage you to say the next prayer. Now that you have accepted Jesus as your Lord and Savior, the next thing you need is to have the power that comes with the filling of the Holy Spirit. This is where you give your spirit a chance to start growing and letting Him allow you to communicate with God on a whole new level. Then, you can start hearing God for yourself.

Congratulations again. Please let me know if I can help you in any way. I love you and am so glad to have you as a loved one in the family of God.

OK, GOD, LET'S START FROM HERE

Prayer for Receiving the Holy Spirit

Now that you are a child of God, your Heavenly Father wants you to have the supernatural power to walk out this new life. When you have the Holy Spirit working in your life, you can enter the presence of the Lord with power. All you need to do is ask, believe, and receive.

Repeat this prayer for the wonderful fulfillment of the Holy Spirit.

"Father God, I ask for You to fill me with Your Holy Spirit. Through my faith, I believe and receive this gift right now. Thank You for coming into my spirit right now. Holy Spirit, I welcome and invite You into my everyday life."

Congratulations! You are now filled with the supernatural gift of the Holy Spirit!

You may not feel any different on the outside, but you are now filled on the inside. Don't let satan try to steal your joy by telling you this was a futile mission. When you prayed that prayer with an earnest heart, you have the Holy Spirit and all of His wonderful gifts.

You may feel strange syllables start to come out of your mouth. Do not be afraid. This is the Holy Spirit speaking through you to God. This is called the gift of tongues. It is meant to build your faith as you speak these words out loud. You may not understand these words in your language, but trust that you are speaking words of life. To learn more about this wonderful gift, read the book of Acts chapter 2 in the Bible.

If you have prayed this prayer, I encourage you to let me know. I would love to rejoice with you and help you anyway I can. Go to my website, www.triciadraper.com and I will help you in any way possible.

Congratulations, and don't ever be afraid of this wonderful gift God has placed inside you. He wants to bless you with this powerful expression of His love.

Versions of the Bible

AMP: Amplified
KJV: King James Version
NIV: New International Version
NLT: New Living Translation

About the Author

Tricia Draper is a published author and resides with her husband and son in Decatur, Texas. She is a leader in her church and has a close personal relationship with God. She has been writing professionally since 1996. She has a certificate from the Institute of Children's Literature. Her genres include children's picture book, fiction for young adults, adult, and woman's inspirational. She and her husband have a ministry online called The Messengers and they encourage you to listen to past messages. You can find out more information on her websites: www.triciadraper.com and www.themessengersradio.com.

CPSIA information can be obtained
at www.ICGtesting.com
Printed in the USA
FSHW010843150319
56307FS